Sea Change

KEITH SPEED

Sea Change

The Battle for the Falklands
and the Future of Britain's Navy

ASHGROVE PRESS, BATH

First published in Great Britain by
ASHGROVE PRESS LTD
26 Gay Street, Bath, Avon BA1 2PD

© H. K. Speed 1982

ISBN 0 906798 20 5

First published 1982

Typeset by Saildean Ltd
Walton-on-Thames, Surrey
Printed by Redwood Burn Ltd
Trowbridge, Wiltshire

Contents

Plates

These will be found between pages 98 and 99

Acknowledgements

I am grateful to all those people who have been helpful to me in writing this book. In particular, I would like to thank Mr Jack Daniel, Warship Director of British Shipbuilders, Ronald Binns, Captain Robin Heath and Major General Ken Perkins of British Aerospace Dynamics Group, Patrick Matthews, Secretary General of Aluminium Federation Ltd, the Secretariat of the General Council of British Shipping, Rear Admiral Martin Wemyss, Vice Admiral Sir Louis Le Bailly, and Mr Tom Bewsey, Director of the British Marine Equipment Council. The House of Commons Library staff are always helpful in providing information for Members of Parliament and have added to the sum of my knowledge which has helped me write this book.

I am particularly grateful for much footslogging research and checking carried out by my son Mark during his University vacation. A very special word of thanks must go to my old friend and fellow globe-trotter Robert Balchin who has provided an abundance of helpful constructive criticism and advice in the production of the final form of the book and has helped turn my sometimes rambling jargon into comprehensible English!

Finally, this book could not have been written without the aid and assistance of Peggy Voss, my wife, who not only typed every word of the manuscript through its various stages, but also dealt with all my constituency correspondence and ran the family as well. In addition, she provided some good down-to-earth criticism which was most valuable.

To all these and many others who cannot be named, my thanks. The opinions in and responsibility for the book are of course entirely mine.

Permission is gratefully acknowledged to reproduce photographs which are copyright as follows:
2. U.S. Navy   3. U.S. Navy   4. Royal Navy
5. U.S. Navy   6. Vickers Shipbuilding/HMS *Invincible*
7. McDonnell Douglas Corporation   8. Hall Russell and Co. Ltd   9. HMS *Endurance*   10. South Eastern Newspapers

1. A Navy Minister Goes— The Big Ships Follow

'Navy Minister Resigns.' 'First Sea Lord May Resign Tomorrow.' 'Defence Issue at Election.'

These were the newspaper headlines that screamed at an apathetic public over a damp February weekend in 1966. I was on my way, as an Officer in the Conservative Research Department, to the Young Conservatives' National Conference when the news broke. Christopher Mayhew, the Navy Minister, had put the matter succinctly in his resignation letter to Prime Minister Harold Wilson: 'I find myself unable to endorse the fundamental political and strategic assumptions of our (defence) policy which have been publicly indicated by Government spokesmen as forming the basis of the (defence) review.'[1]*

His resignation, sent to the Prime Minister on the 17th February, was followed five days later by the resignation of the First Sea Lord, the professional Head of the Navy, Admiral Sir Henry Luce who, with his Service Admiralty Board colleagues, was dismayed that Denis Healey, the Defence Secretary, had axed the new aircraft carrier CVA-01. This meant that the Fleet Air Arm with its fixed wing aeroplanes and big carriers would be phased out in the 1970 s.

There is no doubt in my mind that the events of that February weekend and the battle for the Falkland Islands over sixteen years later are inextricably linked and that the decisions taken as part of the 1966 Defence Review almost certainly made our job tougher in the South Atlantic and led to the certain loss of Royal Naval ships there.

It was a strange twist of fate that Admiral Luce's nephew was to be Minister of State at the Foreign Office in the Spring of 1982 and, with Humphrey Atkins and Lord Carrington, honourably resigned after the Argentinian invasion of the Falklands.

* The numbered references will be found in the section beginning on page 189.

All this was a very long way ahead on that February Saturday and like most young Conservatives I did not possess an early-warning long-range political crystal ball. The Labour Party had just won a convincing By-Election in North Hull, upping their majority from just over 1000 to about 8000; I had been the Research Department 'back room boy' in that campaign and was feeling more than somewhat bruised. There were those, however, who believed that the Mayhew and Luce resignations, the Defence Review, leading to cuts in all the forces, and our slow but steady surrender of bases overseas would help the Conservatives at the forthcoming General Election. I was less optimistic: Harold Wilson had governed for eighteen months with a paper-thin majority. The 'red revolution' predicted by some of the more hard line Conservatives had not come about. The general feeling of the country seemed to me to be that he should be given a reasonable majority now that he had proved himself, and so it turned out. At the General Election in March Labour had 47.9% of the vote, and a majority of 110 seats over the Conservatives.

Thus the British Public, if they knew and cared about the Defence Review and what Mr Healey and his colleagues were doing to the armed forces, certainly did not condemn them. The reputation of the Defence Minister, in retrospect, is usually damaged by Defence Reviews although greater damage is inflicted in the long term on the armed services. The previous major review carried out by Duncan Sandys in 1957 predicted no more manned bomber aircraft and a very great emphasis on missiles. His reputation suffered, perhaps undeservedly, because this was quoted and misquoted against him by opponents in the years that followed.

On taking office sixteen months previously the Labour Government had set a financial ceiling of £2000 millions, at 1964 prices, on defence expenditure that would take place five years later, in the year 1969/70.

It was only after this ceiling had been set that Mr Healey, as Defence Secretary, was allowed to carry out what he called a 'far reaching examination of the Nation's defence needs in the next decade'. This culminated as we have seen in the 1966 White Paper, the withdrawal from overseas bases, resignations and some dramatic reshaping of the Navy. The three large carriers *Victorious, Eagle* and *Ark Royal* would be phased out by the mid 1970s and not replaced.

10

The new carrier, designated CVA-01, would be abandoned, even though a considerable amount of progress had already been made on it and some items with long delivery times had been purchased in readiness. The flexible maritime air power concept would no longer protect our fleet and project our influence abroad.

These decisions followed no fewer than thirty cabinet committee meetings on this particular review and many months of intense lobbying by the RAF and the RN in the Ministry. Wild rumours circulated in defence circles that the gentlemen in light blue were not above altering the maps to ensure that the range of their aircraft was adequate for all eventualities. The gentlemen in dark blue may have been, indeed with hindsight were, right to press for the retention of the Fleet Air Arm as they knew it. Not for the first and certainly not for the last time the Navy did not present its case as well as it might, and the battle was lost. In fact the situation in the short term was to get worse, because on 27th November, 1967 Mr Healey announced a further £100 millions of defence cuts, including the early scrapping of the carrier *Victorious* and the cancellation of eight Fleet Air Arm Buccaneer strike aircraft.

The debate following this important Review saw some very interesting hostages to fortune and revealed the danger of being too specific about anything in the maritime defence field! Thus in his opening speech Mr Healey said: '.... British carriers are not necessary for operations in the Atlantic, Mediterranean or Middle East. It is against the needs of possible operations in the Indian Ocean and the Far East that the case for carriers must stand or fall.'[2] Later in the debate while still justifying his 'scrap the carriers' decision Mr Healey said: 'If we were to take seriously the possibility of landing troops on a hostile shore without allies, outside the range of our land-based aircraft, we would have to have a force of at least five or six carriers so as to be certain of having two permanently available, but such a force, besides costing very large sums far beyond our means, would be far beyond the capacity of the Royal Navy to man. We therefore decided not to keep the capability for such operations, and I regard this as a small sacrifice since we could not afford it anyway and it is difficult to imagine circumstances in which it would be politically wise to use it.'[3] In 1982 of course the small carrier *Hermes* which survived through various defence cuts from her commissioning in 1959 and the smaller carrier *Invincible* were to

11

demonstrate convincingly in the Falkland Islands waters that Mr Healey had been wrong.

Later in the same debate an interesting light either on Mr Healey's briefing, his Ministry's Intelligence or his need for powerful advocacy, I know not which, emerges with the statement: 'Neither the Soviet Union nor China has carriers or plans to have them.[4]

In fact the Soviet Helicopter Cruisers *Moskva* and *Leningrad* had been laid down in 1962 and 1963 respectively and were commissioned in May 1967 and October 1968. Each incorporating a spacious hangar, a flight deck and each carrying up to 18 Hormone anti-submarine helicopters, they showed clearly the way Soviet Naval aviation was going.

They were swiftly followed by the 'Kiev' Class of aircraft carrier, the *Kiev* itself being laid down in 1970 and commissioned in 1975. The *Minsk* was commissioned in 1978 and the *Novorossiisk* in 1981, while the fourth, as yet unnamed, in the class was laid down in 1978 and is due for commissioning in 1983. These carry a mixture of up to thirteen vertical take-off Forger fighter aircraft and nineteen Hormone anti-submarine helicopters. Following them a new 75,000 ton nuclear-powered aircraft carrier was laid down in 1981, and I believe a second one of this class is in an advanced stage of planning. All this is not bad for a country that did not 'plan to have' carriers in 1966!

An early consequential casualty of the cancellation of Britain's new carrier, the CVA-01, was the decision not to proceed with the new Type 82 destroyer. Eight of these were planned but only one, HMS *Bristol*, ever built. This was a brand new design of some 7100 tons powered by a mixture of steam and gas turbine, an early form of Rolls-Royce Maritime Olympus. She had the new medium-range Sea Dart surface-to-air missile system, the Ikara anti-submarine missile, a 4.5 inch gun and was designed for escort work with the now non-existent new carriers. HMS *Bristol* has given a good account of herself particularly since her 1979 refit when she was given excellent communication facilities which enabled her to act as command ship of a task group when required. She nearly fell victim to the 1981 Defence Review (see Chapter Seven), but the Falklands crisis was to end with the rescinding of an order for her premature retirement.

The scrapping of CVA-01 was also a deadly blow to the Fleet Air Arm which in the mid 1960s was accounting for much Naval effort, money and manpower.

For some time before small but far-sighted groups of Naval Officers and designers were sketching plans for a helicopter-carrying cruiser. Their ideas were for a comparatively conventional cruiser with surface armaments forward and a large and uninterrupted flight deck aft capable of operating the bigger new anti-submarine helicopters of the Sea King type then being designed in America. However, this concept, which would have been competing for funds with the proposed new carrier, had not been backed by the Navy Chiefs and the Ministry of Defence and was allowed to become comatose. Ironically, the Soviet Helicopter Cruiser *Moskva* appeared in 1967 and followed closely the ideas of our own designers.

One of the results of the demise of the new CVA-01 was renewed interest in the helicopter cruiser/carrier concept, whilst at the same time the Hawker P1127, later to become the Harrier, was being seen by many navy aviation specialists as an ideal naval aircraft with its vertical or short take-off and landing capability (V/STOL).

The naval staff calculated that a large anti-submarine helicopter with modern sonar and good endurance could have the same anti-submarine warfare capability as a frigate. Five such helicopters on station required a total of nine helicopters to allow for maintenance, repair, flying time etc. They also needed a completely new kind of ship to carry them. This was to be the *Invincible*, first of a new class of through deck cruisers! These had a flight deck extending from right forward to right aft and provision was also made for them to have fixed wing (V/STOL) aircraft on board as well.

The RAF, not unexpectedly in view of Mr Healey's pronouncements in 1966, saw themselves as the sole providers of these fixed wing fighters, and it is said there were suggestions that RAF pilots should fly them from the cruisers. These were not well received by the Navy and not pressed. Due to the persistence of successive Admiralty Boards the order for *Invincible*, first of a class of three 'through deck cruisers', was placed by the Conservative Government in April 1973. *Illustrious* was ordered in May 1976, the third of the class, *Ark Royal*, following in December 1978.

The four Rolls-Royce Marine Olympus gas turbines chosen to power these ships are excellent engines but require vast quantities of

13

air, and much space had to be used in the design for the intakes and trunking into the turbines. Other technical problems, including new design features and complex command and control facilities, delayed completion, and Vickers, who were building *Invincible* as first of the class, had some industrial relations problems to contend with as well.

However, all the changes and delays were by no means detrimental. The capability of the Sea Harriers, which had been ordered for these ships in 1975, was considerably enhanced by a stunningly simple but very clever idea invented by Lieutenant Commander D.R. Taylor RN. He conceived the notion that vectored thrust aircraft (like the Harriers) taking off 'uphill' as it were, on a 'ski-jump', would be able to get airborne at much lower speeds than by taking off from a level deck. The optimum angle of the ski-jump is 20 degrees, which would save 2500lb of payload. Even a 7 degree angle, as fitted to *Invincible*, saves 1000lb which can be used for extra fuel or weapon stores. *Illustrious* has 9 degrees and *Ark Royal* 12 degrees. The old carrier *Hermes* was given a 9 degree ski-jump in her 1980 refit.

Each ship of the 'Invincible' Class today normally carries nine Sea King anti-submarine warfare helicopters and five Sea Harriers, whose role is primarily to fly combat air patrols over the fleet and to intercept long-range shadowing aircraft. Sea Harriers also have an excellent anti-ship capability, particularly when fitted with the Sea Eagle stand-off missile being developed by British Aerospace, and were used as strike aircraft with considerable success in the Falklands War.

The clumsy title 'through deck cruiser' dated back to the 1960s and the aftermath of Healey's 'no more carriers' edict. From then on to mention the word 'carrier' before Ministers, Politicians or the Royal Air Force was tantamount to swearing in church. Thus the absurd fiction was maintained that these new ships were just 'little old cruisers' so nobody need get apoplexy or an ulcer thinking the Navy had ideas above its station. This of course occasioned mirth or puzzlement or both in the real world of the Navy, where a matelot could recognise a small aircraft carrier when he saw one.

Some years afterwards I inherited this situation when I became Navy Minister and while I had no objection to bamboozling the Warsaw Pact, or even on the odd occasion our allies, I did object to fooling ourselves. I reasoned that we had a Conservative Government that believed in carriers and as my good friend Geoffrey Pattie, the RAF Minister, was totally relaxed about it, gave my instructions that in future the 'Invincible' Class should be called Anti-Submarine Warfare Carriers, which is what they are. This was received like a lead balloon in certain sections of the Ministry and the Secretary of State was finally brought in as umpire. After various arguments for and against the carrier title had been exchanged we seemed to reach an impasse. Then I played my trump card. All ships have an identifying or pennant number. This has a letter prefix which is the type of ship. Thus a Cruiser has C and C20 was the cruiser HMS *Tiger*, while an aircraft carrier has the prefix R and HMS *Hermes* is R12. Fortunately some bright gentleman had allocated R05 to *Invincible* some years previously and this already appeared on the ship, in documents, publications and all the other bumph that accompanies the introduction of one of Her Majesty's ships into the Fleet. Faced with this undeniable and irreversible evidence that *Invincible* was a Carrier swan and not a Cruiser duckling these ships are now officially designated as Carriers.

To return from the air to the deep waters of the submarine world, the 1960s and early '70s saw the massive development of our nuclear submarine programme which has continued to this day. The conventional Diesel/Electric submarines, or SSKs, are driven underwater by electric motors supplied by massive electric batteries. This makes them extremely quiet but obviously their endurance and speed are limited by the capacity of their heavy batteries. These have to be recharged by diesel engines, either when the submarine is on the surface or whilst it remains shallowly submerged with a snorkel tube above the water to allow the diesels to suck in air. In either event there is a risk that the surfaced submarine or its snorkel mast can be picked up by enemy radar and the submarine thus detected.

These problems are not present in the nuclear submarines (SSNs or SSBNs) whose propellers are driven by a steam turbine, the steam being generated by a pressurised water type nuclear reactor. These reactors normally need to be refuelled every five or seven years, so the submarines' endurance is normally that of the crew and the food and supplies they can carry. With immense power available the submarines can distill all their own water, provide and condition all their own air, remain underwater for months at a time if need be, and dive to great depths. Their underwater speed, which can be sustained for long periods, varies from 25 to over 40 knots in some of the latest designs. However they are not as quiet as SSKs, all other things being equal, and they are expensive, costing at least three times as much as a conventional submarine and often more.

Submarines of course are potent anti-submarine weapons, detecting, tracking and destroying enemy boats. They can be used for attacking surface ships with torpedoes or missiles. They can lay mines, unseen, in enemy waters. They can be used on clandestine missions to land and recover agents. In their ballistic or cruise missile rôle they can launch nuclear armed missiles of a tactical or strategic kind at enemy land targets from under the sea.

Britain entered the nuclear submarine era in the late 1950s when a British boat and nuclear reactor were under design. The Americans already had the nuclear submarine USS *Skipjack* which was similar to our concept. The 'father' of the nuclear navy in the United States, Admiral Rickover, was rightly jealous of his developments and loath to share them with anyone - most of all with foreigners. Rumour has it there were only three 'Brits' to whom he would talk - the Queen, Mr Macmillan, then Prime Minister, and Admiral Lord Mountbatten, then First Sea Lord. Whether this is true or not, to a lot of people's surprise, an agreement was concluded between Britain and the United States in 1958 for the purchase of a set of nuclear propulsion machinery which was fitted into a submarine laid down here in June 1959 and commissioned in the Spring of 1963 as HMS *Dreadnought*. Much information and design and manufacturing details were exchanged between the USA's Westinghouse Electric and Rolls-Royce, and all subsequent British nuclear submarines have benefited from this original, imaginative and generous agreement.

Dreadnought lasted eighteen years in active service until she was paid off in 1981 and it was announced early in 1982 after much prevarication that she was to be scrapped. I believe the real reason was the future lack of nuclear submarine refitting capacity, since she had a number of years' life left - but of that more anon. She was followed in the years 1967 to 1971 by five more SSNs of the 'Valiant' and 'Churchill' Classes. Some of these were delayed by the parallel Polaris Submarine Programme which was putting a major strain on

16

Vickers at Barrow and Cammell Laird at Birkenhead. The four Polaris submarines (or SSBNs) made up the whole of the 'Resolution' Class. In addition to having six torpedo tubes for their more conventional rôle they carried sixteen Polaris A3 missiles in vertical launch tubes. These missiles, each carrying three nuclear warheads with a range of 2500 miles, have maintained Britain's strategic nuclear deterrent constantly without one moment's interruption since the first Polaris patrol in 1968. At the same time, as far as I am aware, no British Polaris submarine on patrol has ever been detected by a Soviet submarine.

Following this activity nuclear submarine construction continued through the 1970s, albeit at a slower rate, with the completions of a further six 'Swiftsure' Class SSNs at varying dates between 1973 and 1981. The 'Swiftsures' are about thirteen feet shorter than their predecessors, have more advanced equipment and are a knot or two faster underwater. These in their turn are being succeeded by the 'Trafalgar' Class which incorporates further improvements. The first of these was launched in 1981. The eventual aim is to have eighteen SSNs in service, although obviously at any given time a number will be in dock, refitting or refuelling with a new nuclear reactor core. This target of eighteen is more difficult to achieve now that *Dreadnought* is being scrapped and means that over the years nineteen will have to be built. In practical terms seventeen appears to be a realistic new target.

While the Navy was experiencing major changes in policy my own involvement with political and defence matters experienced a sharp change of course with my election to Parliament in the Meriden By-Election in March 1968. The previous well-liked and hard working Labour MP for Meriden, Christopher Rowland, died tragically young in November 1967. The Meriden Conservative Selection Committee short-listed four hopefuls: Sally Oppenheim, later to become MP for Gloucester and Minister for Consumer Affairs; Douglas Hurd, later to become MP for Mid-Oxfordshire and Minister of State at the Foreign Office; Bob Boscowen, later to become MP for Wells and a Government Whip; and myself.

My wife was the only spouse not in attendance at the final selection. She had given birth to our third son Nicholas one week before. In spite of the apparent handicap of her absence I was selected on December 29th and exactly three months later was elected, winning the seat with an 18½% swing.

In the run-up to the By-Election the Public Expenditure White Paper of January 1968 dealt further body blows to the Navy. Aircraft carriers were to be phased out by 1972, not 1975 as had previously been promised; no maritime forces were to be stationed in the Indian Ocean or Far East after 1972; the rate of naval shipbuilding was to be reduced; we were to complete our withdrawal from the Far East and Persian Gulf, again by 1972. Mr Healey summed it up thus: 'I believe that in foreign policy and defence we are now showing a new and necessary realism.'[5] This did not say much for his earlier efforts.

In retrospect I am not sure that I used my new political clout as an MP to best effect in defence matters. I was a keen and reasonably active Lieutenant Commander in the Royal Naval Reserve and rather stuffily conscious of the fact that I really should not take part in defence debates as a serving reserve officer. Thus from March 1968, when I was elected, to June 1970, when a Conservative Government came to power, I watched and quietly ticked about the mismanagement of our nation's defences and particularly the lack of a coherent naval policy. When required I duly voted with my Party against defence cuts but I made little contribution to my own Party's thinking or policies and took no part in defence debates. However I could perhaps have done more in private than I was allowed to do in public.

However, as Lieutenant Commander Keith Speed R.D., R.N.R., MP I suddenly hit the headlines in October 1968. I had been appointed 'additional for training' to HMS *Fearless* for my annual fortnight's reserve service and duly joined the ship late on a Sunday evening at Portland. She is an Amphibious Warfare Assault Ship and has a built-in dock that can flood up to receive or despatch small landing craft, together with a large helicopter deck.

On my arrival I was told we were to do some practice landings off the East Coast of Scotland and then sail for Denmark. It was not long, however, before, instead of sailing East we sailed West to Devonport, disembarked all our surplus passengers and quickly put to sea again on a compass course of West South West, which is a funny way of going from Plymouth to Dundee!

It transpired that we had been ordered to Gibraltar to act as

18

Headquarters Ship for the Prime Minister, Commonwealth Secretary and Attorney General and a meeting place for the Rhodesian talks with Prime Minister Ian Smith and his Rhodesian colleagues. On the passage down the Navy set to work with a will and achieved a rapid transformation of the ship to an elegant Conference Centre, appropriate accommodation being provided for Mr Wilson, the other Ministers and their staffs.

We had no clear guidance or instructions about the Conference until we reached Gibraltar – we did not even know the number of people who would come aboard. The Captain asked me, the only Reserve officer aboard, if I would become his 'political adviser', and inspired guess work together with a great deal of luck ensured that the facilities provided for our guests were appropriate.

The British Press was very amused to discover that an active member of the *Fearless* crew was the recent Tory victor of Meriden. Downing Street did not seem to share Fleet Street's humour because soon after we arrived in Gibraltar I was transferred to complete my training in HMS *Troubridge*, a frigate some distance from *Fearless* and the VIPs!

Whilst Mr Wilson and I were avoiding each other in *Fearless*, design studies were in progress for a new destroyer (Type 42), which was eventually to replace the 'County' Class which had been built in the 1950s as a platform for the Sea Slug surface-to-air missile system. It was made very clear to the design team that Ministers and the Treasury would not entertain a unit cost of more than £11½ millions. To design within tight financial constraints a ship that incorporated the necessary radar, sonar, guns, and the new Sea Dart surface-to-air missile system, plus a flight deck and hangar for the helicopters, together with Rolls-Royce Olympus and Tyne gas turbines to propel it, all meant that sacrifices had to be made. The earlier Type 42s (HMS *Sheffield*, later to be sunk by an Exocet missile in the Falklands, was first of this class) accordingly incorporated all the equipment but the hull was about 30 feet shorter than the designers had wanted.

This shortened hull resulted in a number of effects. First, they were not as good seakeepers as the 'County' Class Destroyers they were to replace or the ubiquitous Leander frigates which were the Navy's maids of all work; in other words they did not ride heavy seas so smoothly or predictably. Secondly, these ships did not have such a large margin of stability as was originally intended. Thirdly, there was no 'elbow room' for expansion or improvement. There was no point during the Falklands operations in talking about fitting new and better close-range weapon missile systems like Sea Wolf to the earlier Type 42 destroyers (such as HMS *Sheffield* and HMS *Coventry* both of which were sunk by enemy action): there just is not the room. Fourteen ships of the class were ordered and the first eight had these limitations. The last six are 42 feet longer, two feet wider and 600 tons heavier. This has improved stability, sea keeping, and speed and has left space for modernisation and improvement.

As I wryly remarked in the post Falklands defence debate, 'One of the early lessons is that in future we must not have ships designed by the Treasury. That is extremely important.'

I have mentioned the Leander frigates. These entered the Fleet over a ten year period from 1963-1972. Their successors were to be the very sophisticated and expensive Type 22 anti-submarine frigates. Because of all the effort on submarines, *Invincible* and Type 42 destroyers there just was not the in-house capacity for the Navy design teams at Bath to do the work in time. So, not without misgivings, a Yarrow/Vosper commercial design of general purpose frigate, the Type 21, was built, and eight were purchased. Comparatively cheap and fast, with a fantastic acceleration from their Rolls-Royce Tyne/Olympus gas turbines, these ships have proved to be extremely popular in the Navy. They are the first choice for Navy Chiefs and Petty Officers to serve in and covered themselves with glory in the South Atlantic although, alas, two, *Antelope* and *Ardent*, were sunk.

The controversial feature of their construction is the extensive use of aluminium in the upper works of the hull. There is no cost saving compared with steel but the weight saving enables the customer to have, for instance, another weapon or radar on board. I shall examine the implications of this later as there has been some fairly uninformed nonsense spoken about the use of aluminium in ships.

To complete this round-up of the new generation of surface ships we have the Type 22 'Broadsword' Class which is the Navy's first all-missile vessel. 'Broadsword' was ordered by the outgoing Conservative Government in 1974. After various hiccoughs due to Mr Nott's naval cuts, orders were resumed, that for number nine of the class being placed in July 1982. Type 22s carry powerful sonar submarine detection equipment and two Lynx helicopters which can be armed with the latest anti-submarine or anti-surface ship missiles. Their anti-surface ship capability is extended by four Exocet launchers and they have been fitted *ab initio* with the excellent short range surface-to-air Sea Wolf missile system. They acquitted themselves very well in the South Atlantic and they have plenty of space. The later ships are longer by some ten metres and allow room for newer weapon systems and special equipment. Their sea keeping is excellent and they have proved that there is no economical substitute for quality.

A feature of all these destroyers and frigates from the 'County' Class onwards has been the helicopter revolution. Starting with the earlier Marks of Wessex in the County destroyers and the lightweight Wasp in the Leanders, the Fleet Arm Rotary Wing department expanded dramatically, so that virtually every major surface ship in the fleet has its own airborne anti-submarine and anti-ship helicopter capability. The replacement of the Wessex by the Sea King and the Wasp by the Lynx gives the Royal Navy as good a team of helicopters, capable of a variety of rôles, as any navy in the world.

All through this time ships were being designed to a price, without the capacity to develop and meet the growing threat. Numbers of hulls, particularly minesweepers, carriers and escort vessels, were diminishing.

However, new weapons, both guns and missiles, new sonars and radars, better electronic warfare equipment and the embarked helicopters were making Royal Naval ships much more effective. New propulsion systems like gas turbines, while not increasing the range of ships, were saving people and space and increasing availability and reliability. Of course the threat, both from the Warsaw Pact navies and other countries in the world, was developing too and so there was never any time when we could rest on our laurels.

Following the leadership given by a series of intelligent First Sea Lords and considerable expertise by the Controller of the Navy (the Admiral on the Admiralty Board who deals with new ships and equipment), ably backed up by immense efforts from the Navy's ship designers, many of the worst effects of the 1966 defence cuts and those that followed in the late 1960s were ameliorated.

But while all this was happening the fleet was losing its big ships and their punch. It was becoming 'short-sighted', because when the three large carriers, *Victorious, Eagle* and finally, in 1978, *Ark Royal* were paid off and scrapped, with them went the Fairey Gannet Airborne Early Warning aircraft. These were turbo propeller aeroplanes of considerable endurance that could fly above the fleet carrying a large and powerful radar set, linked back to the carrier, that could give warning of incoming aircraft or missiles at ranges well in excess of one hundred miles. With them too went the supersonic two-seater Phantom fighters and Buccaneer strike aircraft that gave the fleet its own major air defence and attack systems.

Politicians, Naval staff, NATO planners, the whole defence establishment—all of us—were tacitly going along with the Healey view propounded back in 1966 that the Royal Navy would always operate with friends (the Americans) in the context of NATO and if need be our allies or the RAF would provide the air cover needed and the sometimes essential airborne early warning radar. At the same time there was a trend to design ships and equipment for NATO rather than 'out of area' (i.e. non-NATO) activities. The modern destroyers and frigates had limited ranges without frequent refuelling at sea. Not much emphasis was put on defence against sea skimming missiles, like Exocet, because that was not an area in which the Russians were strong, although a number of countries who were not particularly friendly towards us had purchased these missiles from France. Moreover, since 1966 the wholesale abandonment of British Naval bases around the world had, willy nilly, made us more and more a navy for the North Atlantic, where the major threat undeniably, but not exclusively, lay.

Yet in retrospect it is difficult to understand this capacity for total self-delusion. There was and is ample evidence that Mr Healey's hypothesis, which to be fair to him was largely endorsed by successive governments, was a dangerous one and ignored the Navy's rôle in our national as opposed to NATO maritime interests.

Throughout the 1960s and '70s a series of naval operations including the Beira patrol, Indonesian confrontation, Mauritius, Northern Ireland, the 'Cod Wars' with Iceland, Belize, anti-illegal immigration patrols in Hong Kong and the Gibraltar guardship provided widely differing examples of non-NATO operations where we were or are on our own. However, we finally had to learn the lesson the hard way in the inhospitable waters of the South Atlantic, and British servicemen were to die as a result.

1966 saw not only the start of a major run-down in our maritime capability, which was to be continued under both Labour and Conservative Governments, but also the beginning of the end of conventional aircraft in the Royal Navy, coupled with a doctrine that in future the fleet would always have, when necessary, land based air cover.

The new ships that were designed and built following the review were optimised for working in the North Atlantic with our NATO partners and some were compromise designs due to tight central government financial constraints. We shall see that, at the same time, the Americans started running down their fleets when the Vietnam War ended in 1972. All this was taking place in parallel with the colossal expansion in quantity and quality of the Soviet Navy under Admiral Gorshkov's direction which ensured that by the end of the 1970s it would be the largest the world had ever seen. As I shall show, the response to this alarming state of affairs was for America to reverse her run-down and meet the challenge, while Britain embarked upon still further Navy cuts, beside which Mr Healey's would pale into insignificance.

2. The Soviet Fleet:
26 Years of Expansion

In the period following the Korean War Western Defence Ministers vied with each other in cutting back their defences and particularly their navies; but in Eastern Europe changes of a very different kind were taking place. The Soviet Union was beginning to learn the true meaning of maritime power.

The first recorded naval victory in Russian history was the capture, by a fleet of galleys, of the Turkish Port of Ayor in 1696. The fleet was commanded by a Swiss, Admiral Lefort. He had been appointed by Peter the Great who can truly claim to be the Father of the Russian Navy. Peter realised that there was no great maritime tradition in Northern Russia, either of sea-farers or ship building, but he was wise enough to travel around Europe to try to find men with the sea-going skills the Russians lacked.

During the 18th century Catherine the Great resumed both the expansion of the Russian Navy and the tradition of filling it with non-Russian sea-farers, including many from Britain. John Paul Jones, apart from being an American Naval Folk Hero and giving his name to a terpsichorean form of roulette, finished his naval career as an Admiral in the Russian Navy, joining the fleet two years after the War of Independence in 1778. The Russians have always claimed that his short service with them was undistinguished, for he left Russia in disgrace in 1780 and died in Paris in 1782.

In spite of the Crimean War there were always strong links between the Royal Navy and the Imperial Russian Navy right up to the Revolution in 1917. These included the secondment from time to time of British Officers, the training of Russians in Britain on British ships and a number of joint engagements against the French and the Turks during the first couple of decades in the nineteenth century. Indeed the battle of Navarino in 1825 was a major joint venture between the British, Russians and French who annihilated the Turkish Fleet and thus guaranteed the independence of Greece.

Eighty years later the Imperial Fleet was not so fortunate. Sailing round the world from Libau in the Baltic it met its doom at the hands of the Japanese at the Battle of Tsushima in 1905. The Russians never really recovered from their mauling at the hands of the Japanese, although a new Black Sea fleet acquitted itself well against the German and Turkish forces in the First World War. However, units of the fleet were to the fore in the 1917 Revolution and in February 1918 became under Lenin's orders the 'Socialist Worker Peasant Fleet'. The Revolution, however, did not bring about the hoped-for improvement in conditions in the navy ships or provide a solution to the sailors' grievances. Although the Baltic Fleet had been in the vanguard of the Bolshevik uprising, the politicians, not for the first time and certainly not for the last, took them for granted.

On 1st March 1921 the Kronstadt Mutiny took place. An uprising of sailors in the naval base had early successes against the Republic's loyal soldiers, but after some bitter and bloody fighting the mutiny was crushed and the survivors of the 6000-odd original mutineers were shot. I believe this event, to a greater or lesser extent, coloured the attitude of the Central Committee of the Soviet Communist Party for many years and loyalty to the Party rather than professional seamanship became all-important. This was not helped by Stalin's ruthless purge of middle rank and senior Naval Officers in the 1930s, although at the same time the second Five Year Plan, which started in 1933, incorporated a substantial submarine building programme, so that five years later the Soviet Navy had the largest force of submarines in the world. For much of World War II over sixty of these submarines and over twenty major surface ships which formed the Soviet Pacific Fleet spent their time watching the Japanese with whom they were not at war, and came into their own only in August 1945 when the Russians took over some former Japanese territories.

One Soviet submarine, on the night of 31st January 1945, sank the refugee liner *Wilhelm Gustloff* in the Baltic with the loss of over 6000 lives. For the rest the Soviet fleets were not notable in their activities against the Germans and did little, for example, to help their allies with the bitter and bloody Russian Convoys that sent vital arms and equipment from Britain to the Russian Northern ports. Clearly, during and immediately after the War the Soviet Navy was very much subordinate to the Army and Air Force. For a time, in the middle to late 1940s, it looked as if this would intensify and the international strategic concept of maritime power would not

25

be exploited. In the words of Admiral Gorshkov, 'The first stage, which covers the period of the first post-war decade, saw the building of ships and planes armed with conventional armaments ... The fleet continued to remain at an operational-strategic level, a defensive factor. It continued to be a coastal action fleet....'[6]

From the middle 1950s onwards however all this changed and in a massive naval expansion the Russians began to build an oceanic nuclear missile fleet with significant air, surface and submarine elements, together with a growing chain of world-wide naval bases for repair and anchorage facilities. That this expansion should have occurred under and coincided with the regime of Sergei Georgevich Gorshkov as C-in-C of the Soviet Navy is no stroke of fate but rather a stroke of genius on the part of Nikita Kruschev, who appointed him.

Few British people have heard of Sergei Gorshkov, fewer still know much about him, yet in his achievements, both maritime and political, he is a combination of Pepys, Hawke and Rickover all rolled into one. He was born on 26th February 1910 in Kamenets-podolsk in the Ukraine, was educated at the Frunge Naval Academy at Leningrad, survived the purges of the 1930s and became a Rear Admiral and Flotilla Commander, Sea of Agar and the Danube, when he was only thirty-one. He joined the Communist Party a year later in 1942 and in September of the following year his flotilla covered the Black Sea Fleet and Naval Infantry amphibious assault which recaptured Narovossik from the Germans.

In 1944 he was promoted to Vice Admiral and Squadron Commander of the Black Sea Fleet and spent most of the last year of the War on inshore operations. Promotion to Chief of Staff followed in 1948 and to Commander of the Black Sea Fleet in 1951. He became a full Admiral in 1953 while still in his early 40s. Next year, as a totally trustworthy Communist, he was appointed a Deputy to the Supreme Soviet of the USSR and this was followed in 1955 by his appointment as First Deputy C-in-C of the Navy.

During that year the Commander-in-Chief, Kuznetsov, came under public criticism from Khrushchev who, while visiting the Black Sea Fleet, scornfully dismissed the Soviet cruisers as 'sitting ducks fit only for carrying diplomatic missions to foreign countries'.[7] He subsequently used one, the *Ordzhonikidze*, for his visit to Britain with Bulganin in 1956. It looked like curtains for Kuznetsov and so it proved. A few months later he 'contracted an illness'.

Marshal Malinovsky, the Defence Minister, recommended Gorshkov as a replacement and Khruschev appointed him C-in-C Soviet Navy and Deputy Minister of Defence on 1st January 1956, positions he has continued to hold.

He became a member of the Central Committee of the Communist Party in 1961 and was promoted to Admiral of the Fleet a year later. This continuity of office, something shared by many Soviet ship technologists and designers, coupled with an understanding of and ability to use the Communist bureaucratic and political system, has made him supremely effective in turning his ideas and conceptions into reality.

The idea of the Royal Navy's First Sea Lord writing eleven articles over a period of a year in *Navy News*, the monthly newspaper of the fleet, is a bizarre one, though in recent years I do not doubt that it has sometimes crossed his mind! However, that is precisely what Gorshkov did in 1972-73. He wrote eleven articles entitled 'Navies in War and Peace' in the Soviet Navy's monthly magazine, *Morskoi Sbornik*. In these he argued that a strong and balanced fleet, comprising air, surface and subsurface elements, was of increasing importance as an instrument of national policy in peace, influencing not only the course but the outcome of conflict. Gorshkov made the point that a nation needed a maritime policy and claimed the Soviet Union lacked one. Thus the fleet was of the wrong mix, was designed to be too defensive, and its peacetime international use was far too timid and restrictive.

These articles and the debate in Soviet military and political circles that took place during and after their publication confirmed the importance of a truly maritime policy, endorsed the forward deployment and 'blue water' concept of the fleet and led to the approval of substantial additional resources for the surface warship building programme – the results of which began to be seen from 1979 onwards.

They substantially modified the decisions that had apparently been agreed by the Party Congress for the ninth Five Year Plan in 1971, which the Navy found inadequate.

Gorshkov has been a frequent contributor of articles to the Soviet Press, arguing the Navy's case. He encapsulated his thoughts, philosophy and practice in his book *The Sea Power of the State*, first published in 1976, a major work of over 150,000 words with 120,000

27

copies produced in four years. This book should be essential reading for all who wish to understand contemporary Soviet Naval strategy or philosophy. It is not bad reading for those who want to understand *any* naval strategy and philosophy. A copy was continually on my desk during my second and last year as Navy Minister. Certainly if more NATO politicians on both sides of the Atlantic read it, there might be a much clearer understanding of the Soviet use of sea power and its importance to traditional maritime nations like Britain, the Netherlands, France and the United States, and there might be less talk of reducing naval forces.

Gorshkov sums up the whole ethos of a modern navy on page 247 when he writes:

> Demonstrative actions by the fleet in many cases have made it possible to achieve political ends without resorting to armed struggle merely by putting on pressure with one's own potential might and threatening to start military operations. Thus the fleet has always been an instrument of the policy of states, an important aid to diplomacy in peacetime. To this corresponded the very nature of a navy – constant high combat readiness, mobility and ability in a short time to concentrate its forces in selected areas of the ocean.
>
> In addition, the neutrality of the waters of the world's oceans means that the forces of fleets can be moved forward and concentrated without violating the principles of international law and without providing the other side with formal grounds for protests or other forms of counteraction.

These 'demonstrative actions' have from time to time been the rôle of the Royal Navy, the various fleets of the United States Navy and the Soviet Navy itself. It may be the despatch of a fleet or task force. It may be a single frigate or nuclear submarine as a substantial 'trip wire' with plenty of back-up if needed. Gorshkov believes that the oceans of the world should be regarded as a geographical, political, economic and defence whole. He thus combines not only the Soviet Navy in its world-wide rôle but stresses the importance of the Soviet merchant and fishing fleets and oceanographic research which no doubt will lead to more and more of the recovery of the oceans' mineral wealth.

Fortunately problems of ownership, economic return and other symptoms of decadent capitalism do not cloud the horizon of a Soviet leader!

Gorshkov's political orthodoxy is revealed time and time again in his book and contrasts starkly, for me anyway, with the intellectual honesty of his strategic maritime convictions. Thus on page 150 he both plays down the importance of the Battle of the Atlantic and claims that the Allied victory there was due in no small part to the activities of the Soviet Army and Navy. On the same page he goes on to quote anonymous American and Australian soldiers who apparently sent a letter to Soviet troops saying 'While we were gathering forces for future battles you were fighting and spilling your blood'. This conveniently ignores the fact that the USSR did not enter the war against Germany until 22nd June 1941, by which time British and Australian troops, sailors and airmen had been fighting and shedding blood for nearly 22 months!

The same tunnel vision is applied to the Korean War which Gorshkov lumps under 'Local Wars of Imperialism' and he manages the fairly remarkable feat of describing operations in Korea in some detail without mentioning the United Nations at all. Since as a young midshipman I served in the multi-national UN Task Force that operated off the West Coast of Korea in the months leading up to the 1953 Armistice, I find Gorshkov the hard line communist less convincing than Gorshkov the architect of a modern navy.

Gorshkov came in as the new C-in-C at the end of a post-Korean, post-Stalin policy review. The Communist Party leadership re-assessed the threat from the West as being primarily a surprise nuclear airborne strike. The naval threat, of secondary importance, was seen as nuclear strikes by American carrier-borne aircraft against naval bases, ports and coastal installations. First priority for future naval weapon systems would be long range cruise missiles carried in conventional submarines, aircraft and medium sized surface ships, all operating under Soviet land-based air cover. Gorshkov, as a believer in new technology and a 'missile man', was to carry out the policy changes even if the missiles were still being developed and had not yet been delivered to the fleet.

However Gorshkov was no fool and I believe even at this stage he saw the dangers in too sharply reducing the fleet and its mix,

29

particularly since American technology and capability was developing so rapidly. Accordingly, he made a great show of not building the cruisers in the programme that had not been started—but made equally sure that those under construction were completed. The destroyer and escort programmes were fully completed as well, but the number of conventional submarines built was sharply reduced and research and development on nuclear-powered submarines increased. Replacements for the surface ships were, however, delayed and the shipyard capacity, about fifty per cent, was used for the next few years in building up the Soviet Merchant Fleet, including their formidable fish factory and processing ships which are to be seen in the fishing grounds of the world.

This was putting into practice at an early stage another of Gorshkov's beliefs, that the totality of sea power is to be used for a country's economic, political and defence interests. On page 29 of his book he wrote 'the merchant fleet must be regarded as a universal component of the sea power of a country which has a most important rôle in war and peacetime'.

Back on the naval policy front things had already changed, as it was soon realised that many of the directives issued in the mid 1950s were made out of date by the increased range and capability of the US carrier-based aircraft and the development of the American Polaris Submarine Programme. Gorshkov put in hand a major nuclear submarine building programme, with the aim of doubling deliveries of nuclear submarines to ten a year within ten years, i.e. by 1968. That number was sufficient to give a mix of hunter/killer SSNs and strategic ballistic missile carrying SSBNs. The Soviets saw two major advantages with the submarine-launched nuclear strategic missile like Polaris. First, the invulnerability of the weapon and its launching system, both of which could only be detected when it was too late. Second, in a nuclear exchange Polaris submarines could remain submerged undetected anywhere within their 2500 mile range of target and be subsequently used or their use threatened at a possibly critical stage of the war. The second factor weighed particularly heavily with the Soviets and thus increasingly the Navy found itself involved with the Soviet strategic weapons systems from 1961 onwards.

The first Soviet nuclear powered submarines with an effective strategic missile system was the 'Yankee' Class nuclear submarines which carried sixteen 1500 mile range SS-N-6 missiles per submarine. These became operational in 1968/9. They were complemented and followed by the SS-N-8 4250 mile range missile, twenty of which were carried in each of the later 'Delta' Class submarines. This meant that the missiles could be fired at the United States from Soviet home waters.

In the same way Poseidon and Trident give a vice-versa capability to US Navy submarines. The various marks of Delta came along in the 1970s at a steady rate, to be followed in 1980 by the monster Typhoon of 25,000 tons dived displacement (about twice that of a Delta), built at the huge covered construction sheds at Severodsvinsk. She probably has two nuclear reactors to provide the massive power needed to propel her underwater and to run her systems. She carries twenty SS-NX-20, a new strategic missile with a range in excess of 4000 miles, and a multiple-targeted warhead missile. She is easily the largest submarine ever built and presumably provides a pretty good underwater sonar echo to attacking surface ships, as well as giving heart attacks to sundry whales and sharks!

However, the development of their own sea-based strike capability was only half the equation. Gorshkov understood full well that the Soviet fleet would have to be developed to counter the NATO ballistic-missile submarine threat. The Russians, in other words, would have to get much more involved in anti-submarine warfare.

A number of different types of hunter/killer nuclear submarines (SSNs) have been developed, culminating in the very advanced 'Alpha' Class with a dived speed of forty-two knots, a titanium hull and a diving depth probably in excess of 3000 feet. The costs of these Alphas, which have been slow and difficult to develop, must be astronomical and it is difficult to see it as the good anti-submarine weapon it is presumably designed to be, because it is so large and there is no evidence that it is particularly quiet—an essential requirement when seeking other submarines. However it does show much of Soviet technological research is now being put into submarines. At the same time, surface ships like the anti-submarine destroyers and frigates are being built in considerable numbers, and much development effort is going into satellite and other 'non sound' means of detecting submarines.

Increasingly throughout the 1960s and 1970s Gorshkov was breaking the old defensive concepts and forcing his navy into a forward and subsequently world-wide development. The Soviet Navy essentially comprises four fleets. The largest and most important, the Northern Fleet, is based at Murmansk and has a key Arctic/Atlantic role. The Pacific Fleet, with its HQ at Vladivostock, has grown in importance in the aftermath of the Vietnam War which has led to increased naval activity in the Indian Ocean. The Baltic Fleet, based at Kronstadt, has to traverse the shallow waters of the Baltic to reach the North Sea, which limits severely the draughts of the ships and precludes the passage of submerged submarines. Finally, the Black Sea Fleet, based on Odessa, Sevastopol and Nickoloyev, provides the Soviet presence in the Mediterranean, but has first to pass through the Dardanelles Straits. These are Turkish territorial waters and the Montreux convention limits the passage of foreign warships through them.

To overcome some of these geographical problems, forward bases were needed for the concept of sea control and sea denial to the enemy and for the projection of political and economic power wherever it is in the interests of the Soviet Union so to do. Over the years facilities and anchorages have been provided in Cuba, Ethiopia, Guinea, Vietnam, Aden, Algeria, Libya, Somalia, Angola, the Andaman Islands and Socotra, to name but a few. By 1970 Gorshkov was able to write in *Red Star*, the Russian Military paper:

> The age old dreams of our people have become reality. The pennants of the Soviet Ships now flutter in the most remote corners of the seas and oceans. Our Navy is a real force and possesses the ability to resolve successfully the tasks of defending the state interests of the Soviet Union and of the whole Soviet world.

Of course Gorshkov's path was beset with difficulties. The naval base and anchorage at Valona, Albania, lasted only three years from 1958-61, when Albania left the Warsaw Pact. Similarly, naval base facilities at Alexandria and Port Said in Egypt came to an abrupt end in July 1972 and have never been replaced. But the gains far outweighed these setbacks and there have been dramatic increases over the last two decades in long distance cruises and foreign port visits.

For example, maximum Soviet deployment on any occasion,

including Soviet surface ships, submarines and auxiliaries has grown as follows:

Area	1962	1973	1977	1979
Atlantic	10	25	74	80
Mediterranean	10	96	51	55
Pacific & Indian Ocean	nil	45	56	70

[*Source: Ministry of Defence*]

In order further to project the Soviet power world-wide it was necessary for Gorshkov to put in hand the construction of new nuclear-powered aircraft carriers and battle cruisers. The earlier Moskva helicopter-carriers were designed to operate under land-based air cover. The Kiev carriers are however part of the more powerful surface fleet provided to give essential support to Soviet missile submarines. Their rôle is to deny the Norwegian sea and parts of the North Atlantic to NATO but to secure command of these areas for themselves.

Gorshkov has now put into practice the balanced task group concept. This is a powerful self supporting force of surface ships centred around a major capital ship with great fire power and supported by a mix of modern missile-equipped anti-air and anti-submarine escorts. Each group will have its capital ship, a heavily missile-armed nuclear-powered 'Kirov' class battle cruiser of some 28,000 tons, exercising command and control over the force. This will be supported by a mix of air defence, anti-submarine warfare and anti-ship missile cruisers and destroyers, with two or three cruisers and ten or twelve destroyers for each task group.

A 'Kiev' class carrier will initially provide the close air support, although it is probable that later, when the new nuclear powered aircraft carriers presently under construction become operational, they will provide close- and long-range air cover on the basis of one carrier for every two groups. At 75,000 tons, well armed with missiles and with a virtually unlimited range and endurance, these new carriers will approach the capability of the American nuclear-powered 'super carriers' of the 96,000 ton 'Nimitz' class. They will probably operate naval versions of the existing Soviet Mig 23 or SU24 strike/fighter aircraft plus, I have no doubt, airborne radar and electronic warfare planes.

The Soviets thus have formidable potential and we can expect to see five or six such groups developing at the rate of one (with updated ships) every three or four years. It has been estimated that by the early 1990s, on the known building programme, there will be eight 'air capable' ships, including two new nuclear carriers and four Kiev carriers, five nuclear-powered battle cruisers of the Kirov type, fifteen cruisers, up to sixty-five destroyers and up to sixty frigates. These will be backed up by the powerful new 'Oscar' Class nuclear powered submarine of 13,000 tons dived displacement, armed with twenty-four nuclear SS-NX-19 anti-ship cruise missiles with a 250 mile range!

The land-based Soviet naval force is being re-equipped with new twice-the-speed-of-sound swing wing 'Backfire' bombers as its main strike aircraft, replacing the older 'Badgers'. These, with their 2000 mile range, represent a powerful additional threat. The operational force will probably remain at over three hundred aircraft for the foreseeable future.

I come now to the Russian submarine figures for the coming decade. These depend on the scrapping rate of the older classes of course, but the present building rate of nuclear vessels is very high—one every seven weeks. I doubt very much, however, whether finance and the other resources will allow this rate to be maintained for very long.

Nevertheless, it looks as if by the 1990s long range ballistic missiles subs (SSBNs) will probably have increased to seventy-five or so. Hunter/killer subs (SSNs) will have been reduced to about 110, but these will be of the latest designs and capabilities. The conventional diesel submarines will be around the 80 to 90 mark. The combined British and American submarine forces by the end of this decade, for comparison purposes, are likely to total 48 SSBNs, 116 hunter/killer SSNs and perhaps 20 conventional diesel/electric submarines.

No mention of modern Soviet naval capability is complete without considering its mine-laying potential. It is often forgotten that mines sank more ships in the last War than any other weapon. The Warsaw Pact probably possesses well over half a million mines. These can be detonated by mechanisms which recognise a ship's magnetic 'signature' or its pressure wave, or even the noise of its machinery, or a combination of these methods. The mines can be laid to remain dormant until a certain date or until a certain number of ships have passed (this is known as a 'ship count'). The technology constantly gets more sophisticated and so the techniques of detecting and 'sweeping' them must do also.

Finally, the latter half of the 1970s and early 1980s have seen a resurgence in Soviet amphibious warfare techniques, with massive landing exercises being carried out in the Baltic. Not least among these were the 1981 operations to impress the rebellious and courageous Polish supporters of the Trade Union Solidarity. A new class of amphibious warfare ship (LPD) has been built. Like HMS *Fearless* and HMS *Intrepid* this has a submersible dock which can launch assault craft. The first of the class, the *Ivan Rogov*, became operational in 1978. She is 17,500 tons, can carry up to forty tanks together with a battalion of naval infantry, and has a speed of 26 knots from her gas turbines, faster than *Fearless* or her American equivalents.

The Russian fleet has thus greatly developed its capability to operate world-wide and has the flexibility to show a high or low profile depending on the current political objectives.

I have no doubt that all this expansion is very much the result of Gorshkov's personal beliefs and of his authority. He was particularly convinced that a fleet which had the right balance of carriers, frigates, submarines, destroyers, cruisers, amphibious warfare ships and supporting ships, was of over-riding importance. Thus he writes, 'A stronger but unbalanced fleet may be inferior in its integral operational potential to a numerically weaker but properly balanced fleet', [8] and concludes: 'It may be taken as indisputable that the victories of the fleet and the art of using its forces in any war for which it is created significantly depend on the correct solution of the problem of its balance.' [8]

In fact Gorshkov is developing a more balanced and stronger fleet year by year, and over the period from the late 1950s onwards he and his staff and design teams have built up maritime forces to contain the threat as they perceive it. Many new nuclear hunter-killer submarines, modern anti-submarine surface ships and helicopters paralleled development of new means of submarine detection. New aircraft carriers or air-capable ships, accompanied by powerful nuclear powered battle cruisers, lie at the heart of task groups that can project Soviet power world wide. These are backed up by modern amphibious warfare ships and a mine-laying capability that

35

could threaten the ports and choke points of the enemies of the Soviet Union throughout the world.

Most dangerous of all vessels under Gorshkov's command, however, are the powerful ballistic and Cruise-missile carrying submarines. More numerous and technologically up-dated each year, these nuclear-powered boats can launch, from under water, weapons that can deliver a nuclear warhead with great accuracy at ranges from thirty-five to four thousand two hundred and fifty miles.

Over the past twenty-five years Gorshkov has also appreciated, as many British and American Admirals have not, that politicians and military leaders have first to be educated and then convinced about the importance of maritime power. I find it ironic that in democracies like Britain and the United States the general public needs little convincing and generally has a gut feeling about the dangers of running down the Navy. This does not stop the politicians whom they elect doing just that. In the Soviet Union, where the problems of parliamentary elections are not uppermost in the minds of the political leadership, Gorshkov has over the years achieved a consistency of expansion and a priority claim on resources that would be the envy of a British First Sea Lord or a US Chief of Naval Operations.

Gorshkov delicately got the point across in his book by using the analogy of the French defeats under Napoleon at the hands of the British.

> The actual causes of the success of the English consisted primarily in that onesidedness of the strategy of Napoleon, which stemmed from his fondness for operation in land theatres and a misreading of the rôle of the fleet, the neglect of its possibilities in a war and hence inability to use it in a struggle against a maritime opponent, as was England at that time. [9]

There is, perhaps, a preponderance of Napoleons in some of the upper reaches of British strategic thinking today!

The huge increase in warship numbers has been mirrored by an equally dramatic expansion of the Soviet merchant fleet, for much the same reasons: world-wide projection of Soviet political power. It is also an essential adjunct to the navy, particularly in intelligence gathering and the provision of support facilities for the Soviet fleet in the various oceans of the world.

As I mentioned earlier, soon after becoming C-in-C Gorshkov made adjustments to the naval shipbuilding programme which released more capacity for merchant ship construction. This has been steadily maintained through the past two decades and has resulted not only in a massive increase in numbers and tonnage but a more modern fleet. Two thirds of the ships are less than ten years old; this is several percentage points better than the world average. The Soviet Union has over seventy ports with an annual cargo turnover of at least one million tons while the merchant marine has some thirty ship repair yards to service and maintain the fleet.

But let the figures speak for themselves. In 1960 the Soviet merchant fleet totalled 2,271,000 gross registered tons, about the same as the Danish Fleet and way behind countries like France, West Germany, Italy, Netherlands and Sweden. The UK's merchant fleet in 1960 was 21,416,000 gross registered tons. By 1st July 1981 the Soviet Union's fleet had jumped to 15,724,000 g.r.t., way ahead of all these other countries, while Britain's had only crept up to 24,417,000. The Soviet Union is now the world's second largest owner and operator of passenger liners and is fourth in its number of general cargo ships and fifth in its number of cellular container ships. These formidable statistics, coupled with the modernisation and increasing capacity of the Trans-Siberian railway, pose a threat to Western Maritime interests, a threat which had been taken far too casually until the Falkland Islands war jolted us all out of our complacency.

If anyone still has any doubts about the reasons for the massive Soviet maritime effort let me leave the last word to Gorshkov himself.

> The sea power of our country is directed at ensuring favourable conditions for building Communism, the intensive expansion of the economic power of the country and the steady consolidation of its defence capability. Therefore unflagging attention is being paid to the development of the components of sea power, increasingly resting on the achievements of scientific and technical progress.

At least we cannot say we haven't been warned!

THE SOVIET ACTIVE FLEET IN 1982

Submarines—Nuclear Powered
*SSBN Ballistic Missile Submarines (Yankee, Delta classes) 62
SSBN Ballistic Missile Submarines (Hotel class) 7
*SSGN Cruise Missile Submarines 50
*SSN Torpedo-Attack Submarines 60

Submarines—Diesel-electric Powered
SSB Ballistic Missile Submarines 18
SSC Cruise Missile Submarines 20
*SS Torpedo Attack Submarines 160

Aircraft Carriers and Aviation Cruisers
*CVHG V/STOL Carriers (Kiev class) 2
CHG Aviation Cruisers (Moskva class) 2

Cruisers
*CGN Guided Missile Cruiser (Nuclear) (Kirov class) 1
*CG Guided Missile Cruisers (SAM/SSM) 26
CL Light Cruisers (Sverdlov class) 9

Destroyers
*DDG Guided Missile Destroyers (SAM/SSM) 38
DD Destroyers 30

Frigates (Escorts)
*FFG Guided Missile Frigates (Krivak class) 28
*FF/FFL Frigates/small frigates 140

Small Combatants
*Missile Craft 145
*Patrol/ASW/Torpedo Craft 395
*Minesweepers 395

Amphibious Ships
*LPD Amphibious Assault Transport Dock (Ivan Rogov class) 1
LST Amphibious Vehicle Landing Ships (Alligator, Ropucha classes) 25
LSM Medium Landing Ships (Polnocny/MP-4 classes) 60

Auxiliary Ships
*Mobile Logistics Ships 150
*Other Auxiliaries 605

Source: United States Department of Defense.

* Indicates additional units under construction in these categories.

3.   The West's Response

For two centuries the United States Navy has been 'the Nation's strong instrument of policy in peace and its first line of defense in war', thus declared a great American sailor Admiral Chester Nimitz. Soon after Gorshkov was reassessing and planning the Soviet fleet the US Navy was facing a stern test in the time of the Cuban missile crisis of 1962. Reconnaissance planes and intelligence from Cuba indicated that Soviet long-range missiles were to be installed on the island, together with surface-to-air missile defences. President Kennedy had either to get the missiles removed even at the risk of conflict or alternatively to show up the US as all talk and no action—a veritable paper tiger.

Kennedy imposed a naval blockade of Cuba, euphemistically called a 'quarantine', and Admiral George W. Anderson Jr., Chief of Naval Operations, told the President, 'The Navy will not let you down.' [10] Nor did it, with over four hundred and eighty ships taking part in the operation and the blockade actually starting on October 24th. After a battle of wills Khrushchev backed down and the missiles were removed from Cuba. The US Navy had proved the flexibility and value of sea power in its own backyard.

For most of the rest of the 1960s and early '70s the US Navy, like the United States itself, was preoccupied with Vietnam. The Seventh Fleet was very much involved, with three large carriers usually operating to provide round the clock air operations from the Gulf of Tonkin. The USS *New Jersey*, the last battle-ship in the world to see active service, fired her sixteen inch guns at shore targets. Many cruisers, destroyers, amphibious craft, minesweepers and replenishment ships were involved throughout the conflict.

The Vietnam débâcle brought with it, for a time, a national revulsion against military power and foreign involvement. The doubts and self-questioning I saw when I visited the United States as a newly rejected MP, having lost my Meriden seat at the February 1974 election, were to be reinforced by the trauma of Watergate and

39

the departure from office of President Nixon. During the early 1970s the Chief of Naval Operations, Admiral Elmo R. Zumwalt Jr., embarked on two major initiatives dealing with men and material to modernize the fleet and the Navy's personnel policies.

On the personnel side he issued a series of 'Z-grams' which became famous as instruments of the mini revolution he introduced. Convinced that the US Navy could not stand aloof from the social changes sweeping the country he abolished many minor niggling regulations. He allowed much greater freedom in civilian dress ashore and the length of hair and beards. He encouraged families of crews to join them when their ship was 'homeposted' overseas, and encouraged a more relaxed form of discipline. Efforts were also made to see that the Navy, which had been a predominantly white male service, was made much more attractive to women, blacks and other ethnic minorities. Concurrent with this was the fundamental United States decision to end conscription or 'the draft' and convert to all-volunteer forces. The decision was undoubtedly right but it came at a difficult time in the prevailing mood of the seventies and added to the personnel shortage.

On the material front faced with a worn out navy after the war he made a conscious decision to decommission ships from active service so as to use the severely restricted funds to buy newer and more up to date vessels. Thus by 1972 several hundred ships of all types and sizes had been paid off, leaving the number of ships in commission the lowest since before Pearl Harbor in 1941.

The run-down was not confined to ships. Over the following few years the number of active duty officers and enlisted men declined steadily, and equally worrying was the sharp decline in career re-enlistments. Service men's pay in the US dropped behind that of their civilian counterparts. Some of the racial problems in towns and cities ashore were repeated in the fleet. Some Naval Officers blamed these incidents on the Zumwalt reforms which they claimed had gone too far too fast. Zumwalt was unrepentant and insisted that these problems reflected the tensions that were taking place in the nation as a whole from which the navy could not be insulated. He remained determined to continue the fight for equality of opportunity for all those on the navy's rolls.

Personnel and Weapons Summary, US Navy and Marine Corps 1968-1983

FISCAL YEARS

	1968	1972	1976	1980	1981	1982	1983
			Actual			Planned	
MANPOWER (in thousands)							
ACTIVE DUTY NAVY							
MILITARY PERSONNEL	765.4	588.1	524.7	527.2	540.2	553.0	569.2
Officers	85.4	73.2	63.7	63.1	65.5	67.2	68.9
Enlisted and Midshipmen	680.0	514.9	461.0	464.1	474.7	485.8	500.3
Career reenlistments	26.5	28.4	22.8	21.8	28.6	24.6	23.7
First term reenlistments	14.2	17.1	18.6	19.7	23.0	19.8	33.0
Recruits from civil life	123.4	89.6	83.7	88.8	92.0	83.2	88.8
MARINE CORPS							
MILITARY PERSONNEL (in thousands)	307.3	198.2	192.4	188.5	190.6	192.1	194.5
Officers	24.6	19.8	18.9	18.2	18.4	18.6	19.1
Enlisted	282.7	178.4	173.5	170.3	172.2	173.5	175.5
Career reenlistments	4.9	5.3	5.6	7.6	9.6	8.8	9.2
First term reenlistments	3.7	4.5	4.6	4.3	6.3	7.2	7.5
Recruits from civil life	93.8	56.8	51.2	41.8	36.9	43.0	41.5
PROCUREMENT (QUANTITY)							
SHIPS & CONVERSIONS:							
budgeted	48	24	15	12	20	28	25
Warships only	25	21	9	10	13	10	18
FIXED WING AIRCRAFT:							
budgeted	370	229	232	110	189	207	190
HELICOPTERS: budgeted	286	42	31	15	46	80	98
MISSILES: budgeted	5869	2433	1892	4421	2342	2970	3174

Source: US Department of Defense

While the halving of battle force ships in the twelve years from 1968 and the thirty per cent reduction in aircraft is clear from this table.

US NAVY SHIPS

FISCAL YEARS

	1968	1972	1976 Actual	1980	1981	1982 Planned	1983
TOTAL BATTLE FORCES	957	645	484	479	491	514	535
STRATEGIC FORCES							
Fleet Ballistic							
Missile Ships (SSBN)	41	41	41	40	34	33	34
Support Ships (AS. TAK)	10	9	9	8	7	6	6
Total:	51	50	50	48	41	39	40
BATTLE FORCES							
Carriers (CV. CVN)	15	14	13	13	12	13	13
ASW Carriers (CVS)	8	3	-	-	-	-	-
Battleships (BB)	1	-	-	-	-	-	-
Cruisers (CG. CAG. CA. CC.)	34	28	26	26	27	27	28
Destroyers (DD. DDR)	184	93	31	43	43	43	44
Missile Destroyers (DDG)	37	38	38	37	39	41	41
Frigates (FF. FFG)	50	66	64	71	78	82	90
Submarines (SS. SSN. SSG. SSGN)	105	94	74	79	87	96	99
Patrol Combatants	6	16	8	3	1	6	6
Amphibious Warfare Ships	157	77	62	63	59	59	60
Mine Warfare	84	31	3	3	3	3	3
Mobile Logistics	75	60	48	46	48	51	52
Total:	756	520	367	384	397	421	437
SUPPORT FORCES SHIPS & MOBILIZATION FORCES CAT. A	150	75	67	47	33	54	58
TOTAL AIRCRAFT INVENTORY	9326	7836	6839	6300	6225	6126	6184
TOTAL ACTIVE INVENTORY	8491	6752	5752	5360	5402	5559	5577
IN PIPELINE	1388	1094	821	924	934	666	637
OPERATING	7103	5658	4931	4436	4468	4893	4940
Including Helicopters	1191	1073	1087	1046	1058	1216	1206

Source: US Department of Defense

Through most of the seventies the situation went, for the US Navy, from bad to very bad. The first three budgets of President Carter virtually neglected shipbuilding so that conventional land forces in central Europe could be built up, shades of a policy to be pursued by John Nott a few years later. The main naval rôle as seen by Defense Secretary Harold Brown and his adviser Ambassador Komer was to protect the North Atlantic's sea lines of communication. This was, essentially, a defensive concept in which carriers played little part and which ignored what Gorshkov and the Soviet shipyards were up to. There were also many problems between the navy and the shipbuilders involving delays, claims against each other and cost over-runs. Navy Secretary Graham Claytor and Assistant Navy Secretary Edward Hidalgo, both of whom I came to know well, fought hard to get sense both into overall policy and into sorting out the ship-building problems. They finally succeeded but several critical years had been lost and, for example, in 1979, 1980 and 1981 fewer naval aircraft were bought than were lost through attrition.

By June 1978 alarm bells were sounding off in many quarters. 'Washington Star' comment on 11th June 1978 said: 'Without fanfare or publicity the question of which navy is "No 1"—the United States or Soviet—has been decided. The answer did not come with the recent completion of a second Soviet aircraft carrier, or with the launching last December of a 20,000 ton nuclear-propelled Soviet battle cruiser, or with more than half of the Soviet supersonic backfire jet bombers being assigned to the Red Navy. Rather the decision was made in Washington D.C., when the US Government decided that the United States no longer needed to have sufficient naval forces to support American national goals. This decision was made at a time when the United States is more dependent on the use of the sea than ever before in its 200-year history.'

Fifteen months later on 12th October 1979 Congressman Floyd D. Spence of South Carolina, together with 152 other congressmen both Democrats and Republicans representing Districts right across the country, wrote to President Carter and did not mince words.

The condition of our Navy needs priority attention.... Our

Navy has slipped to a force level of 455 ships, the lowest since pre-World War II. A great number of our ships are not capable of operating in high threat areas, having been designed for escort missions only, while newer, faster Soviet ships bristle with weaponry ... control of the seas and naval projection of power ashore are inseparable.

Thus it was that on 31st January 1980 Admiral Tom Hayward, US Navy Chief of Naval Operations, reporting to the House Armed Services Committee on the Fiscal Year 1981 military posture and budget of the Navy, said: 'Your Navy is stretched thinner today than at any time since the late 1940s. We are being asked to meet increasing demands with a fleet which is roughly half the size it was a decade ago. Individual unit capabilities have increased, as well they must; but geography demands numbers as well as capability, and the simple fact is that today we are trying to meet a three ocean requirement with a one-and-a-half ocean navy.' Admiral Hayward went on to highlight the shortage of skilled Chief and Petty Officers pointing out for example that street cleaners in Southern California earn more than experienced sea-going Petty Officers who work up to thirty hours a week more. He was clearly getting very concerned about the way the Soviet world-wide maritime capability was pulling ahead and was repeating a warning that he had given the previous year.

Admiral Hayward defined the US Navy's role in the 1980s as a three-fold one. First it makes a contribution to strategic deterrence by maintaining a modernised submarine-launched ballistic force. Secondly, it contributes to the deterring of major Soviet aggression in Europe, the Middle East and Asia, by demonstrating that the United States with its allies has a notable capability of reinforcing and resupplying forces opposing the Russians around the periphery of the Soviet Union. This includes not only the reinforcement of the Central Front in Europe but the ability to protect NATO flanks in Scandinavia and the Mediterranean and to support America's friends in the Western Pacific. Thirdly it protects United States interests in the Third World whether they are threatened by the Soviets, their surrogates or by a local power.

In fact the warnings I've already mentioned plus those from

people like Admiral Hayward, Navy Secretary Edward Hidalgo and former Navy Secretary now Deputy Defense Secretary Graham Claytor bore considerable fruit. After the long and wearisome post-Vietnam decline, President Carter on 12th December 1979 affirmed his administration's policy 'to modernise our naval forces and keep them the best in the world'. The President underlined that seapower is 'essential to our global strategy.... in peace and war'. As a consequence he indicated that the future shipbuilding programme would sustain a five hundred and fifty ship navy in the 1990s (an increase of about 20%), adding 'We will continue to build the most capable ships afloat.'

Three months before President Carter gave this commitment I made my first visit to the USA as Navy Minister. Links between British and American Armed Forces have always been strong but I think there has always been a special relationship between the RN and USN and the Royal Marines and the United States Marine Corps. Thus it was that within weeks of my taking office, Graham Claytor the US Secretary of the Navy had invited my wife and me to pay a working visit to the United States, in August 1979. We stayed with Graham and his charming wife Frances at their Washington home, the swimming pool of which sported a Union Flag in our honour during our visit! A former President of the Southern Rail Road, the most profitable of all US rail road companies, Graham has filled his home with superb railway models. He was also the first Secretary of the Navy to have commanded a US Naval ship on active duty.

Just before we arrived he was promoted to Deputy Secretary of Defense but retained his Navy Minister portfolio temporarily until his replacement had been formally appointed. He was also acting Secretary of Transportation whilst a new Secretary was being sought. However he wore all three hats with aplomb and took great personal pains with my programme.

Two highlights stood out. The first was a steam train ride on the footplate of an enormous locomotive with, as far as I could see, everything including the kitchen sink hanging over it. This was on the Southern Rail Road from Charlottesville to Alexandria and I was deputed to whistle the mournful hooter at every crossing as is required by law. We returned somewhat sooty to the large Marine Corps Camp at Quantico where a special display and flight of the prototype AV8B Harrier aircraft, being an advanced version of the current Harrier, developed by McDonnell Douglas and British Aerospace, was organised for us by Jackie Jackson the chief test pilot of the project. The US Marine Corps and the RAF have now ordered considerable quantities of this aircraft. We also saw some young marines being put through their paces and given a pretty tough time by a senior NCO who turned out to be a Royal Marine on exchange duty and who was maintaining the best traditions of the Corps.

The other high point was our visit to Norfolk, Virginia, to meet Admiral Harry Train, USN Supreme Allied Commander Atlantic, and his staff. This is one of the top NATO Commands from where the battle of the Atlantic would be directed and many of the staff are Royal Naval Officers, including Admiral Train's deputy. After a memorable day at Norfolk, including visits to a number of US Navy ships, we flew out next day to the mighty USS *Nimitz* by helicopter. *Nimitz* at 96,000 tons is a very big ship. Her crew totals 6000 including 4 dentists and 6 doctors! She is nuclear-powered and can stay at sea indefinitely. The whole ship is fascinating. There are twenty-four hour snack bars to supplement the normal and very good catering facilities. Rumour has it that one young seaman wrote home after a month saying the ship was great, but only hamburgers for breakfast, dinner and supper was getting 'kinda monotonous'. He had not found the normal dining halls and thought his local twenty-four hour snack bar was the only source of food on board!

The Captain invited me to speak to the Ship's Company through the public address system and I was able to compliment them all on their fine ship and get in a few bull points about the Royal Navy! Then it was time to leave. Unwisely I had speculated at dinner the night before on what it would be like to be steam catapulted from the *Nimitz*—now I was to find out. Aircraft are launched from a conventional Carrier's flight deck for a 'free take off'; they open up their engines, roar down the deck and hope to be airborne by the time they leave the ship over the bows.

The alternative, more usual nowadays, is to attach the aircraft by a strap to a piston which is shot down a cylinder by high power steam, 'catapulting' the aircraft into the air so that it is flying and can climb away from the ship. To assist both these procedures the ship usually steams into the wind at twenty-five knots or thereabouts so that the extra wind over the deck gives the aircraft additional air speed and gets it airborne sooner. It follows that the acceleration from this steam catapult is of the order of two or three times the force of gravity, hurling as it does an aeroplane weighing several tons which starts from rest and which reaches eighty or a hundred knots when it leaves the deck. We were flying in a two piston engine Grumman Cl carrier onboard delivery aircraft, or C.O.D. as it is known, that carries up to seven passengers or freight. The aeroplane was considerably older than the young member of the crew who told us what to do if the aircraft ditched (in practice unless she floated, all you could do was hope your life insurance was paid up and covered this damn-fool activity). We sat 'back to the engine', checked our straps were tight, leant forward so we did not fracture our back or ribcage or both. The engines roared until one thought Mr Pratt would finally part with Mr Whitney, then 'thump'—an acceleration away down the catapult; then 'thump'—a deceleration as our elderly propeller plane finds the catapult has shot her off at a higher speed than the engines give so she drops back in the air. Then we slowly climb away leaving the acres of *Nimitz* flight deck behind us.

When we arrived back at Norfolk air base I noticed Captain Tom Vojtek USN, the normally genial American Naval Attaché in London who was accompanying us, had turned a delicate emerald green colour. 'Your first catapult launch Tom?' I queried nonchalantly. 'Sir, my first and last,' he corrected.

However these interesting and important diversions could not disguise the real problems, particularly on personnel, that the US Navy was facing. Admiral Hayward and his colleagues were brutally frank in our discussions and very interested to hear of our own inherited manpower problems and the solutions we had implemented which, in the late summer of 1979, were beginning to bear fruit. I was told that the Navy was 21,000 Chief and Petty Officers short and that this was affecting the USN's operational capability at a time when they perceived that the maritime threat from the Soviet Union was growing steadily.

I was anxious that the new Conservative Government should be as helpful as possible and it was made very clear to me by members of the Administration and Naval Officers alike that 'out of area' deployments by the Royal Navy, particularly to the Caribbean and Indian Ocean, would help ease the load on the US Navy. They

47

attached particular importance to our long standing experience and traditions of having our ships operating continuously in 'their own back yard', where we have often provided help and first aid against man-made or natural disasters that have hit West Indian islands. Over the next year we were able to meet both these points and give some useful support to the USN.

On 23rd January 1980 President Carter in his State of the Union message made a policy statement which became known as the Carter Doctrine. In it he said: 'Any attempt by any outside force to gain control of the Persian Gulf region will be regarded as an assault on the vital interests of the United States of America, and such an assault will be repelled by any means necessary, including military force.' Although the sentiments were fine this had to be seen against the past neglect and inadequate funding of the 1970s that I have already described.

Five weeks later on 1st March the Rapid Deployment Joint Task Force with a two hundred and sixty-one man headquarters was founded. It has no forces of its own but prepares plans for various contingencies and in a crisis can assume operational command of Rapid Deployment Force Resources taken from any of the four services.

The Rapid Deployment Forces in the near term consists of a number of ships loaded with military supplies and anchored at Diego Garcia in the Indian Ocean. These are designed to support an 11,000 man marine amphibious brigade for a month. In the longer term (to commence in 1984 and be completed by 1987) is the introduction of three maritime prepositioning ship forces, with ships already loaded with stores and supplies positioned in key parts of the world, each capable of supporting an 18,000 man strong marine amphibious group for a month. The idea is that the ships would be moved to a potential problem area and the men flown out from the United States to join up with their heavy equipment. The planning assumes that the landings are not opposed.

All this unfortunately puts a potentially heavy strain upon both naval and support ships and has the disadvantage that specific units are earmarked but not assigned to the Rapid Deployment Force, just as for NATO. I believe the US Marine Corps increasingly will be specifically involved with certain Army units, but if that happens and they are earmarked for NATO as well there is an overall

48

problem of covering all parts simultaneously, particularly on NATO's Northern Flank reinforcing Norway. It seems to me that much of the thinking about the Rapid Deployment Force is right and is in itself a real projection of United States maritime power but there are an awful lot of details still to be sorted out. We cannot take a US commitment to protect Europe and allied interests outside the NATO area for granted.

About the same time as all this was happening, in the spring of 1980, Senators Nunn and Warner were initiating legislation to make real progress in cracking the vexed services pay and allowances problems. The Bill ground its way through the US system and finally became law in the autumn when I was on another ministerial visit to the States. My American friends listened with envy and disbelief when I said we had an Armed Forces Pay Review Board whose annual conclusions were accepted or rejected in whole or part by the Government and acted upon forthwith. The American quadrennial 'review of military compensation' is clearly inadequate. While President Carter appointed a special commission to look at the problem in 1978 and rejected their recommendations to pay cost-of-living increases to the forces in that year and in 1979!

My visit in 1980 was a much longer one and Graham Claytor had been replaced by Ed Hidalgo who became a valued friend of mine. Through the generosity of Admiral Hayward we 'borrowed' his adapted P3 aircraft which provided us with bunks, in-flight movies, excellent food graciously served by navy stewards and a superb flight crew with whom I spent many happy hours chatting and philosophising up forward on the flight deck. We had good discussions with McDonnell Douglas in St. Louis about the submarine-launched Harpoon missile (fired against surface ships from a submarine underwater with a range of about seventy miles) which they would soon be supplying to the Royal Navy and the prospects for the AV8B Super Harrier aircraft which looked good.

On to Seattle and Boeings to talk about naval jetfoils. The Royal Navy was then operating a Boeing jetfoil HMS *Speedy*, which had entered service a few months previously and was doing well in off-shore operations. Unfortunately she was to be paid off and put up for sale in February 1982 in the aftermath of the 1981 Navy cuts.

Flying from Seattle to the naval base of San Diego in Southern California we passed close by the volcano Mount St. Helen's which

49

was still suffering from indigestion. Although we were in a modern pressurised plane we could clearly smell the sulphur fumes in the cockpit. In San Diego we went to sea in a new frigate and had an excellent series of US Navy briefings. I was anxious to get WRNS Officers qualified as pilots starting with communication aircraft and helicopters in Britain. We therefore had an interesting session with two attractive women lieutenants of the US Navy who were qualified and regularly fly to the deck of a carrier as pilots of C.O.D. aircraft. There is still a US statutory prohibition against women serving in combat ships or aircraft. I was convinced that what the US Navy could do, so could the Royal Navy. Alas the increasing budgeting problems, culminating in the Navy cuts, meant that I had greater preoccupations and did not have time to introduce an appropriate scheme but I am sure it will come, and the sooner the better.

The US Marine Corps could not be left out of things and we flew by helicopter inland to their base at Twenty-nine Palms in the California desert. The weather was a blistering 109 degrees Fahrenheit and Brigadier General Glasgow U.S.M.C. invited me to inspect a guard of honour before we set off up-country to witness battle exercises. We moved among the rocks to see Marine Harriers divebombing and strafing with rockets, and armoured fighting vehicles simulating an action in that dusty arid landscape. After test firing some guided weapons on the anti-tank range we went back to the cool dark air-conditioned wardroom for lunch and a surprise public question and answer session on the British political scene.

I got the impression (it was seven weeks before the Presidential elections) that the Marine Officers in deepest California were Reaganites (and Thatcherites) to a man!

This particular visit to the USA was concluded with a visit to a Trident submarine the USS *Daniel Boone* in the Kings Bay Georgia. The *Daniel Boone* had been built to carry the earlier Polaris strategic nuclear missile but had been converted to be fitted with Poseidon and converted again to be fitted with the latest Trident 1 missiles, and I had a most interesting tour all over the boat.

It would obviously have been most improper for me to have got involved in domestic US politics in any way, but my political antennae told me in September 1980 that Carter was going to be a loser. In personal terms I had excellent working relationships with

Graham Claytor and Edward Hidalgo, number two in Defense and Navy Secretary respectively, but in politics, as someone said, a week is a long time.

At the Farnborough Air Show just before my American visit Lord Chalfont arranged a meeting at the Boeing stand between myself and 'a young man called John Lehman who would be President Reagan's Secretary of the Navy'. I don't know where Alun Chalfont got his crystal ball from but it works. I met John Lehman and invited him to my office for a working sandwich lunch next day and we had a good three hour discussion on all things maritime and developed an immediate rapport. He had taken a degree at Cambridge University in 1967. Like myself he was a Lieutenant Commander in the Naval Reserve. At that time he was President of Abingdon Corporation, a management consultancy firm specialising in defence matters. 'When the Governor gets elected,' John told me, 'I shall want you across to continue this discussion, and send some of your naval people so that we can pick their brains on personnel matters.' John was as good as his word. Following President Reagan's election in November 1980, John Lehman was selected by the President to be Navy Secretary on January 23rd and took office on 4th February 1981 as 65th Secretary of the US Navy. Within three weeks he was on the 'phone inviting me to join him and Vice President Bush at the launching (by Mrs Bush) of the new SSN USS *Houston* at Newport News, then to have talks with him and other senior naval people over that long weekend. So private secretary Margaret, capable US Naval attaché Duane Heisinger and I hit the trail once more in the middle of March for the USA where John and I picked up the conversation where it had been left the previous September.

Before the launch and discussions I took part in a memorable wreath laying ceremony at Arlington National Cemetery and presented the Hall of Memory with an Admiralty Board Crest. The launch went very well and Vice President Bush made an excellent short speech to the fifteen thousand strong crowd of men and women shipyard workers and naval personnel, testifying that under the new administration the Navy and warship building were on the move once more. In conversation with the Vice President I found him a charming thoughtful man, very pro-British and very pro-Royal Navy. He had been a naval aviator in World War II and after being

51

shot down spent a long, long time bobbing about in the Pacific until picked up by an American submarine.

As we walked through the salt marshes on the Virginian coastline at the back of John Lehman's weekend escape home he outlined his plans for the expansion of the US Navy. His advocacy for what appeared to be a major change of emphasis in US defence policy from continental to maritime strategy was intellectually honest and appeared, to my admittedly prejudiced view, to be militarily sound.

That Saturday evening we dined well off excellent sea food with some of his naval friends at the Red Snapper, Pago. But nagging away like much more than toothache was the conviction in my mind that, just as the US Navy was, in the nick of time, fully appreciating the Soviet threat and now had an administration determined to do something about it, by a bitter irony Britain appeared to be on the verge of taking steps that would downgrade her own maritime capability and deny the RN the resources needed to meet our NATO and national requirements.

At the end of a stimulating weekend John and his attractive wife Barbara flew back to Washington and I went back to the Newport News Shipyard to be shown around the nearly completed CVN70 the USS *Carl Vinson*, a huge nuclear-powered carrier very similar to the *Nimitz*. This ship, unprecedentedly, was named after a living person, and a politician at that. Carl Vinson had been a Congressman representing a District in Georgia for forty-eight years. For many of those years he had been Chairman of the Standing House Armed Services Committee.

A great man, he ensured that part of President Roosevelt's 'new deal' included a major resurgence in naval shipbuilding. Thus when the United States entered the war the Navy and the shipyards were both well prepared for it. The whole of Vinson's public life was devoted to the defence of his country and the supremacy of its navy. He attended the naming of the 96,000 ton carrier which took place on 15th March 1980 and on that proud day said: 'It is impossible for me to find words to express my gratitude for the high honour you pay me here today. No event in my life, no event in my future can ever equal this day. My cup runneth over, my star has reached its zenith.'

Carl Vinson died at the age of 97 on 1st June 1981 and was thus denied his final ambition, to witness the commissioning ceremony of the ship bearing his name which was to take place in March 1982. The United States and the free world both owe a considerable debt to this great man.

The essence of the Reagan Administration's increase in naval strength is a firm and determined commitment to expand the fleet by approximately thirty per cent from about 470 ships to 600 ships by 1990. The cost in terms of skilled manpower and money is formidable. I estimate that it means an annual ship building programme of about 28 ships at a cost probably in excess of $20 billions a year. But, as Lehman has pointed out, in 1970 defence expenditure was about forty per cent of the Federal Budget, by 1982 it had dropped to twenty-five per cent, and even at the peak of the defence expansion programme for all the services in 1986 it will only reach thirty-seven per cent. Pay and allowances for the Navy are now much more attractive again. Lehman told the Senate Armed Services Committee in his 1982 statement that recruitment for both the Navy and Marines has exceeded one hundred per cent of target while retention of key skilled personnel beyond their normal obligated time has risen strongly from forty-four per cent to sixty-five per cent. Lehman was clearly delighted too that over one thousand skilled and trained former naval personnel each month were re-entering the navy from civilian life.

But if the people problem was on the way to solution, much had to be done to ensure that the ships and equipment would be supplied at the right time, of the right quality and at the right price. Accordingly the new Administration toughened up on its contracting procedures and encouraged a system whereby if time is saved from the completion date or useful economies made in materials the savings are shared. On the other hand, poor performance will land the contractor with an immediate cost burden. This followed the solving of many contractual shipbuilding problems by former Navy Secretaries Claytor and Hidalgo in the previous Administration.

This shift to six hundred ships is also in my judgment a significant shift in US defence policy away from a static continental strategy to a mobile flexible maritime one. Lehman admitted in a broadcast in August 1981 that in numbers of ships the Soviet Union now had the largest navy in the world and it would take the rest of this decade for the Americans to catch up. But Lehman, obviously with the President's backing, is determined that there shall be a

53

three ocean navy for the USA's three ocean commitments and that it will have superiority over Soviet naval forces to ensure control of the sea.

The core of the navy's expansion will be four new surface action battle groups by 1990: at the moment there are none; and additionally three carrier battle groups to add to the present twelve. The surface action groups will be formed around the refitted and modernised battleships *New Jersey, Missouri* and *Wisconsin*. Their nine 16-inch guns can fire a 2700lb shell over twenty-three miles with great accuracy. In addition thirty-two long-range Tomahawk cruise anti-ship and land attack missiles and sixteen shorter-range Harpoon anti-ship missiles will give them a heavy offensive punch. Four fast-firing, radar-controlled phalanx gun mounts will give a reasonably close-range anti-air protection and of course all the radar, communications and electronic warfare equipment is being brought up to date. Their steaming range of over 16,000 miles without refuelling really puts them in the nuclear-powered league for endurance. Interestingly, the cost of modernising the first of these battleships, at $326 millions, is less than the cost of a new US Navy frigate.

The battleship will be able to project power by long-range heavy gun and far longer-range Tomahawk cruise missile while being very resistant to attack and damage. However if a significant air threat exists, either carrier- or land-based air support is required.

The additional three Battle Groups require three extra 'Nimitz' Class nuclear-powered aircraft carriers, to be built after the *Carl Vinson*. The first of the three, CVN71, USS *Theodore Roosevelt* was laid down at Newport News in October 1981 and should join the fleet in the mid-1980s. Two more of the same class will be ordered in 1983, CVN72 and CVN73, to complete the fifteen large deck super carriers. The debate about large versus small carrier has been resolved, as far as the US is concerned, in favour of the large ship. As Lehman points out in his 1982 navy statement to the Senate, 'the large size of the *Nimitz* permits the operation of an airwing with a four-dimensional capability. Action can be taken simultaneously against air, land, surface and sub-surface adversaries. It can operate the entire range of tactical aircraft, both conventional and V/STOL, with the flexibility to adapt to every potential military requirement in the world.'

He goes on to list the other advantages including a large and stable flight deck for safer flying operations, armouring of flight and lower decks and protection of magazines against high- and low-angle attack missiles, multiple provision for protection against torpedoes, over 2000 water-tight and shock-resistant compartments, unlimited range at maximum speed, extensive fire fighting facilities throughout the ship together with protection against chemical, biological and radiation hazards. Where the money is available for administering and running the ships and aircraft, these are powerful arguments since the carriers, as part of a task force, are protected in depth by aircraft, long-range missiles, short-range missiles, electronic warfare measures and close inboard gun weapon systems, as well as a powerful anti-submarine screen of surface ships with both helicopters and conventional aircraft.

Moreover from 1984 the US Navy proposes a new class of multi-purpose helicopter carrier which will have good amphibious assault performance with troop-carrying helicopters and be readily convertible to carry Harrier V/STOL aircraft and anti-submarine helicopters. However they will not incorporate the ski-jump, and the AV8A Harriers do not carry radar and are designed as strike rather than air defence aircraft.

This powerful expansion of carrier and surface battle groups is fully in accord with the philosophy of Mr Caspar Weinberger, US Secretary of Defense, when in his 1982 Report to Congress he warned against the 'fallacy' of a short conventional war. He went on to say: 'The essential purpose of our conventional warfare policy is to prevent war by deterring aggression. Deterrence would be weakened if the enemy were misled to believe that he could easily outblast us in a conventional war.' Later in the report Weinberger is quite explicit. 'Given the world as it is, we must be ready to fight on short notice in a variety of places around the globe, and to carry on the fight until it is won. This means enhancing the readiness, mobility and sustainability of our forces.'

Hence the Battle Groups, the Rapid Deployment Force, the clear and sustainable programme leading to a six hundred ship navy and an increase in general maritime strength. Interestingly, this philosophy, its resulting policies and the political backing for them mirror the philosophy, policies and political will behind Gorshkov and the Soviet Fleet.

The US Navy's powerful surface units need to be supported by cruisers, destroyers and frigates with sophisticated anti-aircraft and anti-submarine sensors and weapons. Four high quality 'Aegis' class cruisers are scheduled to be operational by 1987 with twenty-three now ordered and a total of twenty-eight planned, including a nuclear-powered variant. The Aegis equipped CG-47 class lead-ship is *Ticonderoga* which was christened by Mrs Reagan in May 1981 and is designed with a combination of radars and missile systems to defend carrier Battle Groups against co-ordinated Soviet 'Backfire' bomber raids and anti-ship cruise-missile attacks. The offensive capability of these cruisers includes 'Harpoon' cruise missiles for use against surface ship targets. At £500 millions each these vessels are not only highly sophisticated in their weaponry but extremely costly. The cost however of losing a battle group to air attack would be infinitely higher.

To work with the Aegis cruisers a new class of powerful missile destroyers, known as the DDG-51, is scheduled for construction from the mid 1980s onwards, also to be fitted with the Aegis type anti-air warfare system with an eventual total of sixty-two ships. At long last, the US Navy is also showing interest in the badly neglected area of minesweeping with thirteen new high quality mine warfare ships under way by the new Administration and fourteen single rôle minesweepers planned to start construction in the mid 1980s, while the 'Captor' deep water anti-submarine mine is now available to both the Atlantic and Pacific Fleets.

We should not forget the enormous effort going into submarine construction. John Lehman told me that he believed that the modern conventional diesel/electric submarine was a potent weapon. At the moment however he believes that the US Navy should be concentrating on nuclear-powered ballistic and cruise missile together with hunter/killer submarines over the five financial years up to 1987. The Reagan Administration has increased this to eighteen of the 'Los Angeles' class which will bring nearer the goal of one hundred SSNs, while existing submarines of the class are being retrofitted with vertical launchers for the Tomahawk cruise missile which enables the submarine to still carry its full outfit of torpedoes. Building of the large 'Ohio' class of Trident submarine carrying twenty-four missiles continues at the rate of one a year.

However, even with all this increased nuclear submarine building activity two important points are worth noting. First, the older nuclear submarines are now well over twenty years old and are being scrapped. Second, the average number of US nuclear submarines built in the years up to 1987 will be about two thirds the current Soviet building rate.

The same story of expansion continues with US naval aircraft, where the five-year plan for aircraft procurement submitted to Congress in 1982 was an increase of seventy-five per cent on the previous year. A new total of some nineteen hundred aircraft—peaking to four hundred and forty-two new aircraft in 1987 compared with a low point of only one hundred and twenty-five aircraft in 1980. The Air Arm of the United States Navy apart from the large number of helicopter and modern carrier based aircraft includes substantial numbers of AV8A Harriers and soon AV8B Super Harriers for the US Marine Corps. In addition long range patrol aircraft are operated by the Navy as they are in for example France, Netherlands, Germany and Norway, rather than by the Air Force as is done in the United Kingdom, by 18 Group RAF operating the four Nimrod squadrons.

It is of course a valid argument that it is not just the navies of the USA and the UK that are involved. There are substantial and high quality navies in NATO with perhaps the Dutch and Italians playing particularly significant rôles and Spain is a most useful additional maritime force now that she has become the newest member of the Alliance. In addition, although France is not in NATO, joint exercises and planning with her navy are continuing.

Unfortunately many European NATO countries have had their own budgeting problems and ship replacements have been deferred, new designs delayed and many ageing obsolescent vessels will have to continue in service. This is not to disparage the designs of some of the new ships that are in the West European fleets. I have been greatly impressed by my visits to the Dutch Rolls-Royce powered Kortenaer frigates, two of which are now with the Greek Navy, and the French 'Rubis' Class SSNs now entering service are spoken highly of by submariners and are the smallest nuclear powered attack submarines in the world. I shall have more to say later about the French Navy with its continuing emphasis on conventional carrier-borne aircraft.

However this powerful additional naval armoury of the West is offset to a limited extent by the navies of some of the Warsaw Pact countries and their allies. East Germany has about 140 combatant ships, mostly of modern construction, and its manpower is about 18,000 officers and ratings. Poland has a similar number of ships but about 25,000 manpower strength, although many of its submarines and aircraft are obsolete and considerably older than their East German counterparts. This probably has a great deal to do with the fact that Poland is essentially bankrupt and just cannot afford a modern fleet, even with Soviet aid.

The Rumanian and Bulgarian Navies are both small, and in Bulgaria's case not particularly modern. Countries like South Yemen and Cuba have small but important and expanding navies. Both countries provide strategically important base facilities for the Soviet fleet, and South Yemen occupies a dominating position at the narrows from the Gulf of Aden to the Red Sea.

In a nutshell, therefore, I believe that the reversal of the run-down of the US Fleet has come only just in time. A few more years and the gap in ships, weapons and men would have been too great. In strictly numerical terms, when counting the number of ships on each side, the West still has a numerical advantage in surface forces, though not in submarines. However, as we have seen, there is a constant and growing quality improvement in the offensive capability of the Soviet Navy which makes any straight comparison of total numbers pretty meaningless.

The raison d'être for John Lehman's impressive drive to expand the quality and quantity of US naval forces was admirably summed up by Rear Admiral 'Shap' Shapiro, US Director of Naval Intelligence, when he appeared before the sub-committee on sea power and strategic and critical materials of the House Armed Services Committee on 2nd March 1982 and said: 'The Soviet Navy continues to sustain the unrelenting momentum of new ship and missile programmes aimed at creating a force capable of responding to the full range of war-time and peace-time tasks. We have no reason to expect this momentum to falter. The trends of the past and the evidence at hand suggest that this momentum will continue and perhaps even grow. The implications of this unrelenting build-up of Soviet Seapower should be obvious. The Soviet Navy even today presents a clear and present threat to the vital economic political and strategic interests of the United States and our allies.

Today that Navy is deployed world wide, posing a direct challenge to US prestige and influence in areas critical to our national survival. It is gearing up to play an increasingly important rôle in Soviet defense strategy. It represents a very real and growing challenge that we cannot afford to ignore.'

The results are beginning to show that the US Government, the US Navy and US Industry are meeting this challenge.

4.   The Sun Sets on the Empire

At about the same time that Gorshkov was truly turning the Soviet Navy into a global 'blue water' fleet and beginning to establish a series of world wide naval bases and anchorages, Britain was embarking upon the reverse process. This of course was given a major impetus by the 1966 Defence Review. However, a few days before that White Paper was published and the Navy Minister and the First Sea Lord resigned, the Defence Secretary, Mr Healey, when speaking to the National Press Club in Canberra on 2nd February 1966, said: 'We have no intention of ratting on any of our commitments. We intend to remain and shall remain fully capable of carrying out all the commitments we have at the present time, including those in the Far East, the Middle East and Africa. We do intend to remain in the military sense a world power.'

The decision to withdraw British forces from Aden was announced in the Defence Review of February 1966. In July 1967 the Government announced that Britain would withdraw its forces from Singapore and Malaysia by the mid 1970s but would retain a military capability for action in the area thereafter. In January 1968, in the middle of another domestic economic crisis, the Government announced that Britain would also withdraw completely from the Persian Gulf and the Far East, except for Hong Kong, by December 1971. No wonder Mr Healey ruefully admitted on BBC television on 22nd January 1968: 'I am afraid that a lot of things that many of us have said in the past three years are going to have to be unsaid as a result of the decision we took last week.'

This dramatic reversal of foreign and defence policy in such a short period of time must be seen against the background of the policies of running down the big carriers that could have projected power in different parts of the world irrespective of military bases. So on both the land and the maritime front we really were withdrawing into ourselves rapidly.

60

The withdrawal from Aden was a major naval operation involving up to twenty-five ships including *Fearless, Intrepid* and *Hermes* that were to work together nearly fifteen years later in the Falklands Battle. The evacuation was completed by the end of November 1967. With the rise of Arab nationalism and the collapse of the new British-backed Federal Government in Aden it was probably inevitable that we should finally have to give up all hope of retaining use of the port and the refuelling facilities, the airfield and the barracks. However, the People's Republic of South Yemen, as the territory is now called, is a most useful Soviet base at a strategic position dominating the entrance to the Red Sea. Apart from providing the Soviet Fleet and Air Force with the facilities Britain used to use, it is also home for some 2500 Soviet 'military advisers', 800 Cuban 'advisers' and over 300 from E. Germany. At the same time the island of Socotra, which lies 200 miles to the south and is also South Yemeni territory, is used as a secure anchorage by Soviet naval and merchant ships.

The withdrawal from Bahrain in the Persian Gulf was completed on July 15th 1971 when the Heath Conservative Government was in office. HMS *Jufair*, the naval base in Bahrain, was closed down, and for the first time for decades the Royal Navy no longer had a presence in the Gulf. 'A Treaty of Friendship' was signed with Bahrain one month later. To be fair to Mr Heath, while Leader of the Opposition he had told Parliament on 18th January, 1968, 'When the time comes—and on the Prime Minister's time schedule the opportunity will be open to us—we shall ignore the time phasing laid down by the Prime Minister and his Government for the Far East and the Middle East. We shall support our country's friends and allies and we shall restore the good name of Britain.'[11] In fact there was no strong pressure from these 'friends' for Britain to remain in the Persian Gulf.

On 1st November 1971, some seventeen months after the Conservatives' election victory, the Singapore naval base was formally handed over to the Island's government which had gained independence in 1965. In January of the previous year, speaking at Bristol while still Leader of the Opposition, Mr Heath had suggested that a Commonwealth Force should remain in Singapore and Malaysia after British forces withdrew. A British/Australian/New Zealand presence called ANZUK did remain in token form but this was finally wound up by the Labour Government under Harold Wilson after winning the 1974 election.

However on the positive side it was in 1971 that the decision was taken to develop Diego Garcia in the Indian Ocean from a small Anglo-American communications centre into a large naval and air operating base. That development, started in the mid 1970s, continues.

Back in 1955 Britain and South Africa concluded an agreement over the regional defence of South Africa against external aggression. The agreement included details of the defence of the sea routes around the Cape and the transfer of the Royal Naval base at Simonstown to the South African government. However this transfer was subject to Britain being allowed to continue to use the facilities of this base at all times; allies of Britain would be allowed to use them in war time. The Commander-in-Chief South Atlantic would continue to fly his flag at Simonstown and exercise command over Royal Naval units in and around South Africa. Additionally he was designated C-in-C of a maritime strategic zone and he would be responsible for naval war planning for Britain and South Africa. The emphasis was very much on combined training and co-ordination between the two navies.

In January 1967 negotiations took place between the two countries following the British Government's decision to abolish the post of C-in-C South Atlantic and withdraw the frigate that had permanently been on station in the area. The result of this was greater responsibility for the South African Naval Chief of Staff, but the Royal Navy would have continued use of the Simonstown facilities. However, soon after the Labour Party won the 1974 General Election Mr Callaghan, who was then Foreign Secretary, reimposed the embargo on all arms sales to South Africa. The South African Defence Minister, Mr P. W. Botha, later to become South Africa's Prime Minister, reacted angrily and asked if Britain intended to honour its responsibilities under the Simonstown Agreement. The answer came within a few months, on 20th December 1974, when the Prime Minister told Parliament that Britain did not regard the Simonstown Agreement as operative any longer.

Thus at a stroke Britain denied herself the only fully developed naval base on the African coastline with sophisticated maintenance and docking facilities. The Western allies are not exactly over-endowed with naval facilities in Africa and the attempted coup in Kenya in August 1982 must put a question mark over the continued use of Mombasa as a port for British and American ships serving in the Indian Ocean. However, international politics being what they are I have no doubt that we shall carry on denying ourselves any South African naval support facilities, get no kudos for so doing, and rely upon the small South African Navy and Air Force to keep an eye for us on the strategically vital Cape route to the West.

The withdrawal from foreign bases was continued by the decision in the Labour Government's 1975 Defence White Paper that forces were to remain in Malta until 31st March 1979, when the Military Facilities Agreement expired, and all British forces and ships would be withdrawn by that date. In fact under Mr Mintoff's brand of Maltese Socialism there had been a feeling for some time that we were not the most welcome of guests, but when the Navy sailed out early in 1979 they severed links spanning several centuries. This had followed the decision announced by the Government in 1975 that, from 1st April 1976, there would be no British maritime forces assigned to the Mediterranean in support of NATO. Although the Conservative spokesmen denounced this at the time there is no longer any permanent Royal Naval presence in this area and, just to make doubly sure, John Nott announced in the Autumn of 1981 the closure of Gibraltar naval dockyard and a running down of the military facilities there to save ten million pounds gross a year, about the cost of four Lynx helicopters!

Thus several governments have resolutely pursued the withdrawal of United Kingdom forces from various strategic areas over the years. Usually the decision has been made by Labour Governments but often the execution has been by Conservative ones. If we were a small Continental power I have no doubt that this would make economic sense and we should be hastily withdrawing into a 'fortress Europe', but we are not. We still have important mercantile interests throughout the world that may at any time need protection.

We still also have a considerable number of small states or territories for whose defence we are responsible. These include Saint Christopher and Nevis (St Kitts and Nevis) in the Leeward Islands, which has full internal self-government, but the United Kingdom retains responsibility for defence and external affairs. The situation is similar in Brunei in the East Indies where the UK continues to be responsible for her external affairs and to consult with the Brunei Government in the event of external attack or threat of such attack. To these we must add the dependent territories of Anguilla, Bermuda, British Virgin Islands, Cayman Islands, Montserrat, and the Turks and Caicos Islands in the Caribbean, plus British Antarctic Territory, the Falkland Islands and Dependencies and St Helena and Dependencies in the South Atlantic, together with Gibraltar, Hong Kong, British Indian Ocean Territory and the Pitcairn Group in the Pacific. In addition, there are special arrangements for Britain to come to Belize's aid should Belize face external aggression; these were agreed between the two governments just prior to Belize's independence in September 1981. The interesting thing about this list is that, apart from Bermuda and Gibraltar, all the other countries are out of the NATO area and they still represent a residual debt from the palmy days of the British Empire, a debt that we have to be prepared to honour as the Falklands crisis has shown.

For Britain and the West generally there are a number of vital maritime bottlenecks or 'choke points' as they are called which, if closed or disrupted, could swiftly threaten our trade. The first one is the Cape of Good Hope around which, the South African Government has calculated, 600,000 tons of shipping a day pass to and from Western Europe. Yet the South African Navy, which has been depleted by the sad accidental sinking of the frigate *President Kruger* in February 1982, is too small and lacks modern ocean-going anti-submarine forces to protect this area. There is no guarantee that such protection is given the requisite degree of priority by the South African Government, even though Soviet submarines have often been reported exercising in the sea routes around the Cape.

We then have the Bab-el-Mandeb at the southern entrance to the Red Sea effectively bounded by South Yemen and Ethiopia. The Soviet fleet is a constant visitor both to Aden in the South Yemen and Massawa 200 miles north in Ethiopia. With the improvements made to the Suez Canal, tankers loaded up to 150,000 tonnes can now pass through it and thus through the vital choke point at Bab-el-Mandeb. Already nearly 20,000 vessels a year use this route. Around the corner is the Strait of Hormuz, the narrow entrance to the Persian Gulf boarded on one side by that most unstable of countries—Iran. As Rear Admiral Shapiro, Director of United States Naval Intelligence, reminded Congress in March 1982:

> A successful naval closure of the Strait of Hormuz—in connection say, with a Soviet military intervention in Iran —would shut off fifteen million barrels of oil a day to the West, representing over sixty per cent of United States, Western Europe and Japanese imports and causing a yearly loss ... of over one and a half trillion dollars from combined Western economies.

American, French, British and, occasionally, Australian ships have been patrolling the Strait of Hormuz and the Gulf of Oman since the Iraq/Iran war started in 1980.

The Straits of Gibraltar control the narrow entrance to the Mediterranean and through them pass an average of 125 surface ships a day. No-one knows the number of submarines travelling through here or any of these key 'choke points'. The countries flanking the Straits, Morocco and Spain, with the British Territory of Gibraltar, are not likely to come under Soviet influence. Indeed Spain's membership of NATO in 1982 will add to the security of these waters. Only nine miles wide however at the narrowest breadth, they are susceptible to mining or other forms of blocking, notwithstanding the strong tidal currents which flow through.

In Asia there is the Malacca Strait which is used by most vessels going to and from the Far East and where there is an average daily flow of about 160 ships. The countries bordering the Strait are Singapore, Indonesia and Malaysia, and none of these nations has the resources to provide all the patrols and protection necessary, not least because of the problems of modern sophisticated piracy that exists in the Andaman and South China and Java Seas. Large draught ships, drawing over 20 metres, go down the west side of Sumatra and then turn through the Sunda Strait between Sumatra and Java. This is of course all part of Indonesia, and the same limitations on patrolling and protecting this route apply as to the Malaccan Strait. The Soviets have a major naval base at Cam Ranh Bay several hundred miles north in Vietnam.

The interesting thing about all these choke points is that they are all in areas where Britain had naval bases from which she has since withdrawn or is withdrawing. This should not surprise us. Our forebears were not stupid and based the fleet in the best positions to give help and support to our territories, investments and shipping companies when they needed them. Thus to safeguard these areas we had bases at Simonstown, Aden, Bahrain, Gibraltar and Singapore respectively.

Back in 1968 Admiral Tom Moorer, then Chief of Naval Operations of the United States Navy, put forward an initiative which never really got off the ground, not least because of the negative response from Britain and other countries. His proposal was that representatives of those countries adjacent to the great global choke points should have a preliminary meeting at the US Naval War College in Newport, Rhode Island. They should try to work out a series of possible naval exercises directly related to intimidation in those areas. I think Admiral Moorer hoped that a general consensus would emerge that those points were the vital strategic areas in the Western Alliance, and that Britain and America might jointly discuss, with the governments of the countries concerned, political approval for some form of contingency planning, regular exercises and an agreed command and control structure.

Perhaps Admiral Moorer was ahead of his time. Certainly the US was still pre-occupied with the Vietnam War and many countries did not see what Gorshkov's expansion plans were to achieve. There is no such excuse in the 1980s. Britain can either try to leave all this kind of planning to the Americans, a move that will be resisted there both by the politicians and by the United States Navy, or we can ignore the threat and hope it will go away. This seems to be the philosophy behind the 1981 defence policy! I believe that we must start seriously to consider the possibility of local maritime alliances with countries such as the US, Spain, the Netherlands, France, Kenya, Oman, Bahrain and the Gulf States, Bangladesh, Singapore, Malaysia, Indonesia, Australia, South Africa and Japan. Enlightened self interest is emotionally powerful and intellectually respectable and this is a situation where such a motive could be the spur for the West to take the initiative to safeguard our world-wide interests, rather than supinely react with too little, too late, to the Soviet build-up.

5. The Civilian Fleets

The great American admiral and naval historian Alfred Mahan has wisely noted that 'A nation's maritime commerce strength in peacetime is the most telling indication of its overall endurance during war'. The eyes of this country focussed on our merchant fleet during the Falklands War and there came suddenly a realisation that the merchant navy was our fourth arm of defence and that without British merchant ships the South Atlantic operation, or any other like it, would have been impossible. As the *Queen Elizabeth II* and *Canberra* and *Uganda* resumed their cruising activities, as the tankers and cargo ships went back to their peace-time routine, memories began to fade and we started to take our merchant fleet for granted once again. Whether we like it or not however we are a trading nation with world-wide interests and investments. Notwithstanding the immense efforts of our farmers, much of our food and all our tropical produce is imported. We, together with Western Europe, import considerable quantities of key commodities such as copper, tin, chrome, bauxite, manganese, potash and iron ore to name but a few. Ninety-five per cent of all our imports, and a similar proportion of our exports, travel by sea, most still in British merchant ships.

Rudyard Kipling's famous poem is still particularly relevant to us as a nation.

> Send out your Big Warships to guard our Big Steamers,
> So no one can stop us from bringing your food.
> For the bread that you eat and the biscuits you nibble,
> The sweets that you suck and the joints that you carve,
> They are brought to you daily by all us Big Steamers—
> And if anyone hinders our coming you'll starve!

The importance of merchant shipping in reinforcement and resupply across the North Atlantic in times of tension or war cannot be overestimated. Even if the maximum number of troops and equipment can be 'prepositioned', in other words be ready for action in their appropriate European theatre of operations, ninety per cent of reinforcements and additional supplies will go by sea and will involve about one million men, eleven million tons of military equipment and seventeen million tons of petrol, oil and lubricants. There are of course people who have argued that any war is likely to be of short duration and confined to the Central Front of Europe.

If that argument is true then of course reinforcement and resupply, the shipping to carry it, the naval ships and aircraft to escort it—all are unnecessary. I am quite certain however, as I have already mentioned in passing, that the United States Defense Secretary was absolutely right to have warned in his 1983 Fiscal Year Report to Congress: 'Another fallacy in recent defense policy regarding conventional warfare has been the "short war" assumption—the notion that in planning our strategy and designing our forces we could rely on the assumption that a conventional war would be of short duration. Common sense and past experience tell us otherwise.'

Thus, in times of both peace and war Britain has powerful reasons for needing a large and varied merchant fleet. I have already shown how the Soviet fleet has expanded at a much higher rate than those of Western navies. If we look at the number of British ships, other than tankers, we find that in the ten years 1971 to 1981 there has been a reduction from 1356 to 720 general cargo ships, a reduction from 28 to 10 passenger liners, a reduction from 234 to 189 dry cargo ships and very slight increases in container ships (51 to 59) and ferries (73 to 75). The manpower situation is equally alarming. The number of British Merchant Navy Officers fell from 41,000 in 1975 to 28,000 in 1982, and UK ratings numbered 38,000 in 1975 and only 26,000 seven years later.

Part of this run-down in both ships and manpower is due to the considerable disparity in manning costs between say an Asian manned ship and one with an American or West European crew. In total it costs a West European shipowner, not operating under a 'flag of convenience' and employing seamen from his own country, about three times as much to crew a dry-bulk carrier vessel of, say, 30,000 tons as it does an Indian, Singaporean or Hong Kong shipowner using his own nationals. Officers working for Western shipping companies are usually paid full time, whether they are at sea or not; this is not the case, however, with many non-European companies where officers are paid on a 'voyage-only' basis. Although modern merchant ships are highly automated, not least to save manpower costs, there is a limit below which the size of crew must not drop if the ship is to be navigated and handled safely by qualified people.

Thus the British Merchant Marine, with indeed those of a number of other NATO nations, is under attack on several fronts. It has to compete with lower manning costs and lower taxes from third world countries not concerned with the same high standards. The world recession of the late 1970s and the early 1980s has brought particular problems for merchant shipping which faces competition also from the Soviet block who use shipping or railways as a tool of economic warfare or a means of getting foreign currency. Commercial charges to make a profit, or at least to cover costs, are disregarded. At the moment this country is idly letting the laws of supply and demand take over and slowly, but quite definitely, our national merchant fleet is disappearing.

A major assessment of our national need for a merchant fleet in time of tension or war should be carried out at once by the Department of Industry, Department of Trade and the Ministry of Defence. New tax measures should be carefully considered, such as new ship investment allowances to give incentives to profitable companies. In addition, ships fitted with certain defence equipment could qualify for a special revenue payment to keep the equipment in working order and the crew trained to use or maintain it. This equipment could come under the authority of an enlarged Royal Naval Reserve which British merchant seamen could be encouraged to join and so receive appropriate pay and special allowances. What I believe is clear is that fresh thinking is required, and the problem is much more urgent than most people realise.

These ideas for defence equipment can apply both to existing vessels and newly constructed ships. The General Council of British Shipping in the wake of the Falklands battle has put forward some positive ideas that are well worth pursuing. Certain merchant ships could be fitted with anti-missile 'seducers' which can shoot 'chaff' (metallic strips) into the air and deceive a missile into thinking the 'chaff' is the ship so that it passes harmlessly by. Special container-ised air-defence missile systems like Sea Wolf could be fitted to certain larger ships so that they can have high quality protection against the threat of air attack. Container ships, bulk carriers or tankers could have simple decks with 'ski-jumps' put on them so that they can provide additional platforms for jump-jet Sea Harriers or anti-submarine helicopters. The actual control and direction of these aircraft would normally have to be carried out, however, by a suitably equipped naval warship. Joint work on such a concept between Britain and the United States, the ARAPAHO project, has been languishing mainly because of lack of funds. It must be revived.

Merchant tankers above a minimum size should be fitted with the appropriate gear, hose connections etc., for refuelling other ships at sea. A number of tankers had to be fitted with this equipment in a great hurry for the Falklands battle—next time there may not be time. Equally it makes sense at the building stage of a ship to construct appropriately strengthened decks which can be used as helicopter platforms or for mounting missiles and guns.

Finally I do not exclude some special types of ships being jointly funded by shipping companies and the Ministry of Defence. Such ventures could include ocean-going roll-on/roll-off ships. This funding might also cover the installation of special lifts in, say, car ferries so that aircraft or other large equipment could be quickly moved and parked below the main deck. It is often forgotten that the Royal Navy has its own 'merchant fleet', the Royal Fleet Auxiliaries, manned by civilians, and these should be used to test the concept of arming merchant ships. At the moment the numbers of RFA vessels are being cut down as quickly as possible to save money.

It is however no good projecting our mercantile presence if all British owned ships finish up being built in foreign ship yards and fitted out with foreign equipment, because we have killed off our own industries in this field. For a considerable number of years the shipbuilding industries in many countries throughout the world have been protected from foreign competition by a series of devices including straightforward subsidies, subventions, non-tariff barriers, and good old bureaucratic procrastination. Ship building of course is not just a job for ship yards. On an average merchant ship, about sixty per cent of the value of the vessel is supplied by contractors of services and equipment, and for every shipyard worker there are three others working in the marine equipment companies.

Matters in Britain came to a head with the replacement of the containership *Atlantic Conveyor* which was hit by an Exocet missile and abandoned on 25th May 1982. Her Master Captain North and a number of her crew were killed. Cunard, the British member of the Atlantic Container Line consortium which owned her, had sought tenders for a 35,000 ton successor to the lost 15,000 ton ship. Japanese and Korean shipyards quoted prices that were widely believed to be heavily subsidised by their respective governments. The prestige value of obtaining the replacement order for the ship lost in combat was considerable, but nevertheless it seemed for a while that we would be daft and masochistic enough to let it go to one of our main international competitors. Members of Parliament of all parties in the House of Commons took a very dim view indeed of this important order going abroad, especially as the four other new ships in the consortium which were to be ordered, one by the French partner and three by the Swedish company, were to be built in their own countries with the help of special government subsidies.

Finally agreement was reached here that there would be a significant government contribution and the shipyard, Swan Hunters of Tyneside, would pull out all stops to deliver within the price and on time. I normally hate subsidies as they can mask inefficiency and conceal the true price of a product. In the case of merchant ship building, where everyone is in on the act and competitors are quite ruthless in getting financial help from their governments to undercut British industry so as to obtain a job, and then perhaps finally drive us out of business, it seems to me we do not have much option. I cannot believe that it is in the national interest to have to rely upon foreign firms for ship building and marine equipment. Perhaps one day there will be truly fair international competition properly maintained and enforced; being of a cynical frame of mind I personally will not believe it until it happens.

Chartering is another way to help the shipbuilding industry—and the Navy at the same time—and it can also help to sidestep some of the financial blocks when money is very tight. In 1980 while I was Navy Minister there was a need for a new 30,000 ton tanker to replace one of the twenty year old tankers of 25,000 tons displacement still in service. Cammell Laird of Birkenhead had submitted a very competitive tender and badly needed the work. There was not the money available in the Navy budget to pay for the new ship which would not take too long to build. But a deal was arranged whereby the ship would be built for civilian owners who would then arrange a long term charter to the Ministry thus spreading the financial load. This meant a reasonable profit for the Charter Firm who had got the deal in a competitive market. It meant a good contract for Cammell Laird who had won the order. It meant a brand new purpose built tanker, to be named *Bayleaf*, for the Royal Fleet Auxiliary and the replacement of a much older ship which was more costly to run. Finally it meant that the Ministry could spread the cost over a large number of years. I think that this method of financing the building of Royal Fleet Auxiliary ships should be considerably extended. There is nothing new about 'leasing' or 'chartering', and it is another way of helping both the shipbuilding industry and the merchant fleet that supports the Navy.

Before Treasury purists and other peace-loving souls hold up their hands in horror at such an aggressive role for maritime capitalism, it is worth a quick glance at the way the Soviets are developing and operating their merchant fleet. As well as expanding in numbers over the decade from 1971, their merchant ships have increased their calls to Third World ports by sixty per cent over the same period. The addition, during the1970s, of forty roll-on/roll-off ships which can load and unload cargoes via large ramps has increased the capability of the USSR to deliver military cargo such as tanks and armoured personnel carriers to ports without sophisticated cargo handling facilities. It has helped their merchant marine to deliver Soviet weapons to client states both routinely and in times of tension. This type of ship could at any time support Russian naval amphibious operations. We should not forget that the Soviet merchant fleet is really the equivalent of the Royal Fleet Auxiliary in that a high proportion of its tankers and cargo ships provide logistic support and backup for the Soviet Navy on a world-wide basis. It also includes some six hundred extended range, high speed dry-cargo ships with built in cranes capable of lifting armoured vehicles suitable for amphibious warfare. Many merchant ships are manned by members of the Soviet Naval Reserve and contain much military communication and other equipment.

It is a strange irony that as the Soviets are establishing more naval bases and anchorages around the world and thus adding to the seaborne support of their fighting ships, Britain has been steadily withdrawing from foreign naval bases and dockyards and at the same time steadily reducing its seaborne logistic support which could have replaced them.

Gorshkov in his book reminds us: 'The fishing fleet (in its widest sense) is a constituent part of the civil fleet and an important component of the sea-power of the State.' [12] The Soviets practise what they preach, possessing easily the world's largest fishing fleet of vessels of 100 gross registered tons or more. In 1981 their fleet totalled 3694 such boats with a total tonnage of 3,691,427. Japan was next highest with 2900 boats but a tonnage some way short of one million tons. The United Kingdom, by comparison, owned 473 boats with a total tonnage of 143,752. The important point about the Soviet fleet is the high proportion of large truly ocean-going trawlers. The largest, those of four thousand tons or more, were operated by only three countries in the world in 1981. Japan has eight, South Korea has seven and the Soviet Union has thirty-eight. Similarly, in 1981 there was a world total of 1164 ocean-going trawlers and fishing vessels between 2000 and 4000 tons. The Soviet Union possessed no fewer than 855 of these, the United Kingdom none.

The trend in the ten years up to 1981 has been for the Soviet Union to increase by several hundred its number of fishing vessels, but more importantly to increase the total tonnage by fifty per cent. In other words their boats are getting much bigger, more self-supporting and they are emulating the 'blue water' capability of the Soviet navy. For example, in 1971, the USSR had only four trawlers over 4000 tons and 530 between 2000 and 4000 tons. The UK's fishing fleet has gone in precisely the opposite direction, from a total of 579 boats to 473 in the ten years before 1981 and has dropped from a tonnage of 238,000 down to 143,752. Although UK trawlers in the 1000 to 2000 ton class have marginally increased over that period from twenty-nine to thirty-five, the long range 500 to 1000 ton boats have dropped from one hundred and twenty-seven to nineteen.

British fishing vessels traditionally have kept their fish frozen or chilled on board and brought the catch home for processing so we have not needed to operate fish carriers or fish factory ships. The Soviet Union on the other hand has for many years used these ships to follow their fishing fleets around the world; they can process the catch on board so that it may be marketed for human or animal consumption or as a fertiliser. In 1971, the Russians operated 455 such ships out of a world total of 587. In 1981 that had risen to 563 out of a world total of 844 including 116 massive Soviet factory ships of 10,000 tons and above.

The Soviet fishing fleet is of great economic importance. It provides about twenty five per cent of the USSR's protein and earns, or saves, foreign currency. The Russians export to third world countries a considerable amount of fishing equipment and sophisticated processing plant and have entered into arrangements with a number of nations to help them develop their own fishing industries. Their trawlers, now operating on a world-wide basis, act as important intelligence gatherers for the Soviet Navy. Their rôle ranges from simple reporting of Western naval and merchant ship movements to the most sophisticated and complex electronic information collection. The array of wires and aerials normally to be seen on a Russian trawler is not there simply to improve the reception of the crew's favourite television programme!

In addition, logistical help is given to the Soviet Navy by this world-wide fishing fleet, and particularly the factory ships, wherever and whenever required. Backing up this great enterprise is a modern advanced fleet engaged on hydrographical and oceanographic surveying and research into the wealth of the sea. There is of course a critically useful spin-off from this oceanography in the field of submarine and anti-submarine warfare including the charting of underwater routes for the new generation of deep diving Soviet submarines.

I believe all this has happened because the Soviets, particularly Gorshkov and his political masters, have grasped the essential truth that maritime strategy is an indivisible one. All the components, naval and merchant shipping, fishing and research, shipbuilding and ports must be seen in a total, if flexible, framework. For a country that has, or aspires to have, world-wide interests, it is essential that the component parts be encouraged to work more closely together so that the whole is greater than the sum of the individual parts.

In Britain, and many other countries, for a variety of historical and economic reasons the fishing industry has declined in terms of tonnage, size of ships and availability of new equipment. Obviously the Soviets have an advantage with a domestic market five times the size of Britain's. The extension of territorial or national fishing limits, coupled with an increasing economic nationalism, have affected our fishermen in many of their traditional long distance fishing grounds. Britain's membership of the EEC, which I wholeheartedly support, has meant sacrifices and adjustments in certain specialist areas. Having said all this, the harsh fact remains that in the ten years since 1971 such diverse countries as Canada, France, Norway, Panama and Poland have overtaken us in total gross tonnage of fishing vessels of one hundred tons and over. Equally disturbing is the fact that of the fishing vessels over eighty feet long registered in UK ports on 31st December 1980, nearly two thirds were over ten years old and over a quarter were over twenty years old.

I believe the fishing industry in the UK, like the merchant shipping industry, has been treated in isolation and without sufficient regard to its long term importance and future. The Whitehall administrative set-up does not really help. The Royal Navy comes under the Ministry of Defence, the Merchant Navy is now under the Department of Trade, but fishing is under the Ministry of Agriculture, Fisheries and Food. Shipbuilding however comes under the Department of Industry. The Scottish, Northern Ireland and Welsh Offices all have a fishing interest, while fishery protection is the responsibility of the Ministry of Defence, the Ministry of Agriculture and the Scottish Office which indeed runs some of its own fishery protection boats.

The Treasury's extraordinary accounting rules mean that the Ministry of Defence has to charge the Ministry of Agriculture full costs for the Navy to fly airborne fishery protection patrols or to mount similar sea-based ones. The Ministry of Agriculture finds that a private firm can fly such a patrol cheaper or that the Scottish Office can do it cheaper with a vessel manned by a civilian crew because they are not having to pay the overheads which the Royal Navy has to include in its costings. However, the taxpayer does not save any money because Naval or RAF aircraft still have to fly to allow the aircrew to get so many flying hours in. Fishery protection ships still cost money whether they are alongside in Rosyth dockyard or out at sea catching poachers, and their crews have to be trained too.

This naive lack of corporate approach which in so many ways, not least in the 1981 Defence Review, would cause a commercial accountant to raise his eyebrows will steadily undermine any coherent attempt at a maritime programme suited to our needs. Soon Britain will depend on the Russians, Norwegians or Japanese to catch its fish and will let Fleetwood, Grimsby, Hull, Lowestoft, Aberdeen, Peterhead and the other fishing ports close down. Let us be clear that if we do that a key part of Britain's maritime strategy also disappears, for the fast conversion of trawlers to minesweepers or other vessels of war (a significant factor in the Falklands campaign) will be impossible because none will be left. When we engage in negotiations internationally on fishing catches, both with the EEC and with individual countries, we should always be tough and have these important strategic truths at the backs of our minds. Much more needs to be done to draw the strands of the different departmental and ministerial interests together. This vital duality of commerce and defence, if allowed to dwindle away, could severely impair Britain's economy and its security.

6. And Now I Am the Ruler of the Queen's Navee!

Wednesday 28th March 1979 was the eleventh anniversary of my entry to Parliament. At 3.34 that afternoon Mrs Thatcher rose and moved the motion 'That this House has no confidence in Her Majesty's Government'. Twenty-six speeches and six and three quarter hours later that motion was carried by a majority of one after high drama concerning the whereabouts and voting intentions of certain Northern Ireland MPs. The Prime Minister Mr Callaghan immediately announced that there would be a general election. It was with a sense of eager anticipation that I joined my friends and colleagues Reggie Eyre (Hall Green), Hugh Rossi (Hornsey) and Marcus Fox (Shipley) in our shared tiny room optimistically called an office.

All of us had important party jobs in opposition and all could reasonably expect a ministerial appointment if the Conservatives won. (In fact Marcus was made Under Secretary of State at the Department of the Environment, Reggie Under Secretary at Trade, and Hugh Minister of State for Northern Ireland.)

Obviously the first priority was to be re-elected but I had an excellent and experienced agent in Ashford, who was a close personal friend, a first class team of constituency workers and was defending a majority of 6000, so although taking nothing for granted, I felt confident that I would win. The following day I went off to the West Midlands to speak for another good friend, Hal Miller the Conservative MP for Redditch and Bromsgrove. It was while I was in Hal's constituency office on the afternoon of Friday 30th March, that I heard of the stunning and tragic news of Airey Neave's killing.

It is now said by many people that they can remember precisely what they were doing and the sense of shock they felt when they heard of President Kennedy's death. That is certainly true for me and applies also to the deaths of two other people: Airey Neave, a dear friend and colleague (I was his whip for nearly two years), and tragically, five months later, Lord Mountbatten on that fateful Bank

Holiday weekend when he and other members of his boat party were foully murdered.

However life had to go on and so did electioneering. Since November 1977 I had been Opposition Spokesman on immigration and race relations, under the wing of Willie Whitelaw, who was Shadow Cabinet Home Office spokesman. This had meant a series of fascinating visits over sixteen months to the heartlands of Bolton, Southall, Brixton, Leicester, Birmingham, Liverpool, Lewisham, Slough and many other places. Fortunately I am extremely fond of curries and pepperpot soup and Red Stripe beer and have a cast iron digestive system, because invariably my Asian or West Indian hosts were warm and generous with their hospitality. My prime task during the early part of this period was to draw up a credible Conservative immigration policy that could be accepted by not only the Tory Party but the British public at large. Once such a policy had been agreed by the Shadow Cabinet then there was a major 'selling' job to do with the ethnic minority groups many of whom were, understandably, suspicious about our policy and our motives. These suspicions were often, alas, fanned into flames of racial fear or hatred by extremists mostly of the Left, sometimes of the Right, who set out quite deliberately to distort our policies.

Thus during the Election campaign itself I made tours of constituencies in London, the East and West Midlands and Greater Manchester speaking for our candidates in areas where there was usually an important ethnic vote. We won all the seats which I visited except those in Greater Manchester, so I was not displeased with my activities.

All this meant that before the Election while in opposition I was so busy as a Home Affairs spokesman that I had little time to take a detailed interest in defence. But, perhaps even more important, as a serving Officer, a Lieutenant Commander in the Royal Naval Reserve, I was not allowed to blast away at the then Labour Government's defence policy. In these matters I was a Naval Officer first and an MP second—quite rightly. Added to which I had a sub-conscious phobia which made me fear that if I took part in a defence debate I would blurt out secret information that I had acquired during my naval reserve training and jeopardise some aspect of naval security.

Thus it was that I was not fully aware of a veritable deluge of warship orders by the outgoing Labour Government. On the 27th March 1979 HMS *Gloucester*, a Type 42 destroyer, had been ordered from Vosper Thorneycrofts in Southampton. A month later on the 25th April, just a week before the General Election polling day, two Type 22 frigates, HMS *Boxer* and HMS *Beaver*, were ordered from Yarrows on the Clyde in Scotland and two Type 42 destroyers HMS *Edinburgh* from Cammell Lairds at Birkenhead on Merseyside and HMS *York* from Swan Hunters on the Tyne. I am sure it was a pure coincidence that there were marginal seats close to all these ship-yards! It is of course one thing to order ships but another thing to pay for them. Since a large warship takes four or five years to build, the act of placing a series of orders at the end of a Government commits the next to ongoing capital expenditure that can pre-empt a budget to a large extent and limit the freedom of action of successor ministers, as I was shortly to find out.

I have had plenty of time since April 1979 to reflect on this buying spree and my own view is that it was wrong for a number of important reasons. Firstly when Parliament has been dissolved and the Government is within eight days of a General Election and certainly the possibility, if not the probability of losing power, it is wrong to tie up money and specific classes of ships in this way. An alternative administration, after time to consider its priorities, might not want to order this number of surface ships at all, or certainly would wish to consider a different mix of types. (With some, but not too much, hindsight I would have ordered the one destroyer HMS *Gloucester* but the other four ships instead of being two destroyers and two frigates would have been four Type 22 frigates.)

Secondly to order ships bunched in this way means a similar bunching on payments and exacerbates the cash outflow problems of the Ministry. There is I believe much to be said for getting nearer the Dutch system where a larger number of one type of ship can be ordered, thus getting the benefits of lower unit costs but on a phased production and delivery basis. If a foreign navy then wishes to buy a frigate it can be allocated one from an appropriate stage in the programme and an additional order for the home navy tacked on at the end so they do not lose out.

Thirdly I sincerely doubt the wisdom of placing large public sector orders eight days before an election when those orders clearly could have substantial political consequences locally for good or ill, and the whole operation is being financed by the taxpayer. I believe once an election has been announced by the Prime Minister there should be a moratorium on all further substantial public contracts whether for ships, aircraft, roads, hospitals or whatever.

Anyway election day finally dawned. I am told there are parliamentary candidates who like and enjoy the 'Count'. They are probably in the same category as those who start every morning with a ten-mile jog followed by a cold bath or keep tarantulas to control the fly problem. I do not belong to this eccentric band. The fact that I have, in my heart of hearts, known to within a 1000 or so my majority or minority at every count I have been to does not in any way lessen my distaste for them. Fortunately I have always fought elections where the local government officer running the count has been efficient and his staff swift so that the affair has not been unnecessarily prolonged. The night of 3rd May 1979 was not only the count for the parliamentary election but it was also the count for the local council borough elections too. The great British Public who take complicated football pool permutations in their stride found these elections relative child's play.

At about 1 a.m. I was declared elected with a majority over my Labour opponent of some 13,000 and a satisfying swing of nearly eight per cent. By this time it was clear nationally that Mr Callaghan and his Labour Government had lost and Britain was returning a Conservative Government under the first ever woman Prime Minister, Margaret Thatcher.

In the days following a General Election MPs of the winning party have the air of men who have filled in the winning line of the treble chance but cannot remember if they have posted the coupon. The more deceitful ones put on a pose that it does not matter too much anyway.

First the key cabinet appointments are announced, then the still important but lesser ministerial posts, then a clutch of parliamentary under-secretaryships, then the bits and pieces down to assistant whip. (I was for a time the most junior assistant whip in Mr Heath's Government in June 1970.) While all this is going on, one finds elaborate reasons never to be far from a telephone. Or in casual terms you leave strangely precise details of your itinerary on visits to the library, the garage or the village shop.

So it was on Sunday afternoon 6th May while enjoying Vernon

Handley conducting the Guildford Symphony Orchestra playing Rachmaninov's Second Symphony in the Stour Centre, Ashford, the Manager quietly beckoned me out and told me the Chief Whip wished me to ring him. Excitement—disappointment; the more senior and responsible jobs are put to the would-be Ministers personally by the Prime Minister, while the Chief Whip handles the lesser positions such as Parliamentary Under-Secretary of State. Michael Jopling, the new Chief Whip, came straight to the point. Yes it was a Parliamentary Under-Secretary of State's job, but in the Ministry of Defence, as one of the Ministers in charge of the Army, Navy or Airforce, working under Francis Pym. It didn't take too many micro-seconds for me to decide that all these propositions were agreeable so the answer was 'Yes'. The details I sorted out with my new Secretary of State, Francis Pym, later that night, and it was settled that I would take over the Navy, Geoffrey Pattie the RAF and Barney Heyhoe the Army.

Our political system is such that it was not until much later it dawned on me that my four years as an Opposition Spokesman first on local government then on immigration and race relations bore little relevance to my new portfolio. However my four years at Dartmouth, ten years in the regular Navy and twenty-two years in the Naval Reserve should have prepared me for the challenge I was about to undertake.

Within two hours of my agreeing my responsibility with Francis Pym my telephone rang and my new private secretary introduced himself over the 'phone. We had a useful discussion and arranged to meet on the Tuesday morning 8th May, following the Bank Holiday Monday.

In my ministerial experience from 1972-74 and again while in the Ministry of Defence I was fortunate in my private office staff, for not only were they efficient, loyal and prepared to work unearthly hours when necessary, they were all very nice people as well. A Minister's private office is his link with the outside world, other departments and private offices in his own ministry, and other ministries in Whitehall. The private office filters the mass of correspondence, reports, minutes and other bumf without which no large-scale organisation can operate today. The Minister's correspondence, his busy weekly schedule, his briefings and the necessary material for parliamentary speeches, questions and the like are all arranged there. A good private office, and mine was good, will act as an early warning system to alert their minister to problems or obstruction over his policies or new directives from on high or outside the department, that may very much affect what he is trying to do.

The problems in the Ministry of Defence private offices were compounded by the fact that not only are its staff dealing with other ministers and civil servants, but they are dealing with people from all four services as well, ranging in rank from Admiral of the Fleet, down to a Leading Steward. This calls for tact, patience and understanding on behalf of all concerned, but in my experience given the right people it does work. My office had a Principal Private Secretary who was a higher executive officer who would be promoted to principal on the next job, an assistant p/s who was an executive officer, a Second Officer Women's Royal Naval Service, who ran my diary, organised my travelling arrangements and helped out wherever and whenever required. The team was completed by the clerical officer and typists in the 'outer office' and my Royal Marine Driver, Steve, who became a valued friend, adviser and confidant, in our many hours together in the official Ford Granada.

At this time when we still had a separate Minister for the Army, Navy and Airforce each private office had its own Service Officer who apart from running the diary or whatever could give advice on service matters and was a most valuable 'service input' into the civilian team. The Army and Airforce had a major and squadron leader, the Navy always had an attractive second officer W̄RNS and I took great pains to see that the Senior Service maintained this tradition!

When my private secretary whom I had 'inherited' from my predecessor moved out on promotion to another challenging job I interviewed a number of likely well qualified young civil servants as his successor. Apart from all the usual questions one query I had to put to each of them was 'Are you prepared to jump out of a helicopter at a great height and be lowered to the ground on a wire, and are you prepared to be transferred between two fast moving ships at sea by means of a jackstay?' To their credit all candidates gave an unequivocal 'Yes', but this was a genuine question, as Margaret, who got the job, found out.

Often when travelling around the fleet a jackstay transfer is the normal means of getting from ship A to ship B while both are steaming along. This means you are ferried across from one ship to another suspended in a strop that is attached by a pulley to a line that runs between the two ships. It's rather like those fascinating cash pots that used to zoom around on wires in old fashioned family drapers. The alternative is to fly in by helicopter usually landing on the ship's flight deck. However some ships are too small or cluttered to have such luxuries. Then it is a question of a strop over the shoulders and under the arms which you hope is attached to the winch wire and you launch yourself into space to be received on what is usually a heaving and rolling deck many feet below.

To leave the ship means standing on the self-same heaving deck while the helicopter roars and vibrates above you. Strop over shoulders and under armpits and up you go saying a quiet prayer for Westland who built the helicopter and Rolls-Royce who made the engine. When you near the machine you are sure you are going to be winched into the rotor blade which is revolving at about three times a second. However, you never are and somehow you scrabble through the open door and contrive to look unconcerned!

In Northern Ireland while visiting Royal Marine Commandos I have seen tough provost sergeants go an interesting shade of pale green when learning that for security reasons we should be 'descending on the wire'. They only really recovered when my attractive and undeniably feminine private secretary departed with great aplomb and experience like the old hand she was becoming, and male chauvinist pride forced them to follow suit!

After the private office the Admiralty Board was the organisation that loomed largest in my life. Although the Secretary of State was *de jure* Chairman of the Admiralty Board, *de facto* it was the Navy Minister.

Its members then included the First Sea Lord (the uniformed professional Head of the Royal Navy, whose office was next to mine), the Vice Chief of Naval Staff (responsible for all operational aspects of Board policy including fighting strategy and tactics, operational requirements of ships and weapons) and the Chief of Fleet Support (responsible for the dockyards and stores with logistic back-up plus modernisation and repair of ships, weapons and equipment).

Also included were the Controller (responsible for the ordering and design of ships, weapons and equipment) and the Second Sea

Lord (responsible for naval personnel matters, conditions of service, pay, recruiting etc.).

All these posts were filled by serving Admirals or Vice Admirals. In addition there was the Navy's Chief Scientist, the Deputy Secretary who was the Civil Service Head of the Navy and the Second Permanent Secretary who is responsible for administration within the Ministry of Defence and who sat on all three Service Boards. Finally I was in the chair as 'primus inter pares.'

Board meetings tended to be somewhat formal affairs to endorse and note papers that had been circulated beforehand. They took place in the historic boardroom of Admiralty House with the wind gauge on the wall and the whole building rustling with memories of Nelson, Churchill and other great heroes of the past. This is not to say that lively and constructive discussions did not take place, but inevitably much work was done at the frequent informal meetings we all had with one another. However the Board provided an opportunity for the three wings of the Navy Management, Service, Civilian and Political, to come together and sometimes for one group to put a point of view to the others in a discussion that could be very frank but was always without rancour.

In the spring of 1981, when we were agonising over Mr Nott's proposed Navy cuts, we had a series of 'informal' Board meetings in my office. These were marathon affairs which tested the patience and endurance of everyone. At the prompting of Lynda, my Wren personal assistant, we broke with tradition, or rather started a new one, by serving 'Horses' Necks' (brandy and ginger ale) or 'Buck's Fizz' when we felt we were getting near screaming pitch. I don't know if it improved the discussion but it helped our morale!

My biggest problem in May 1979 however was that NCOs and Officers were leaving all the services in dramatically large numbers. This was jeopardising our manning of sea-going ships in the Navy and was due to the previous Labour Government's folly in allowing service pay to drop far behind its civilian equivalent (just as the Americans had been doing). Within a week of taking office we fully implemented the independent review body's pay award of thirty-two per cent and thus restored 'comparability'. This eventually stopped the rot of people leaving prematurely and stimulated recruiting which progressed very well until 1981, when it was severely restricted and service redundancies were announced as part of the

Navy cuts. However the immediate crisis meant that in June I had to tell Parliament that we were putting five older frigates and the helicopter cruiser *Blake* into reserve because we just did not have enough of the right kind of people to provide their ships' companies.

The Royal Navy and Royal Marines were my prime responsibilities but pensions for all the armed services came under my wing as well. This was a minefield that could trap the unwary. There were and are many unfairnesses and anomalies in service pensions, where the amount received can depend critically on a particular date of retirement. If the hapless servicemen gets it wrong by a month or two he can lose a lot of money. Identifying the problem is easier than solving it; however one of my earliest tasks in this field was immensely rewarding and proved a number of points.

By a quirk of historical accident the widows of men of Warrant Officer rank and below, in all the services, whose husbands had retired with a service pension before September 1950, received no pension when the husband died. In other words the pension died with him. This did not apply to anyone of any rank who retired after that date, or Officers who retired before it. Successive Governments had, apparently, grappled with this problem for years without success.

The 1979 General Election Manifesto said that the Conservative Government would right this wrong, so the problem fell into my lap. I assembled a small but keen group of civil servants from the pensions department of the Ministry and after we had agreed the outlines of a possible scheme I asked them to go away and work out the details. Their target date for starting the scheme was Armistice Day—i.e. less than six months. They responded cheerfully and intelligently to the challenge, and the detailed scheme plus a major publicity campaign was delivered well in time. I ensured that my ministerial colleagues in other departments were content for us to go ahead, including of course the Treasury and to the one or two doubters I played the trump card of 'Manifesto commitment' which did the trick. The scheme was launched on time and today 25,000 elderly widows are now receiving a service widow's pension which previously had been denied to them. Perhaps as important was the self-respect and esteem they felt at being able to share the pension their late husbands had earned by service (normally at least 22 years) to the Crown.

The points thus proved were firstly that our civil service directed properly is resourceful and can usually come up with the right answer. Secondly, a 'manifesto commitment' is a magic password to unlocking other departments' doors. Thirdly, anything that involves spending money—and this scheme only cost a few million pounds—should be done earlier rather than later before the Treasury battens down the hatches!

In fact money, or rather the lack of it, was to be a recurring problem that finally blossomed into a full-blown nightmare, two years later. The difficulty, and it is faced by every defence ministry in the world, is that 'defence inflation' is much higher than ordinary inflation, because equipment becomes more advanced and increasingly reaches into the realms of very high technology. It is much more effective than its predecessor and in many cases has a performance undreamed-of even a few years ago. Alas its cost reaches undreamed-of levels also. Thus a new Hunt Class Mine Counter Measures vessel currently costs about £35 millions. This is a comparatively small vessel of 685 tonnes built of glass-reinforced plastics. By contrast the Type 42 destroyers of six times the size cost £12 millions when the first one was built in 1974.

However all this means that to increase defence expenditure each year by three per cent more than ordinary inflation, which is the NATO target accepted by the government, is still to go backwards, since defence inflation has been probably overall five per cent more than ordinary inflation. In other words you need an annual increase of inflation plus five per cent in your defence budget to keep up to date.

Costly ships and aircraft were not the only problem. Weapons too become fantastically expensive in order to meet the threat from the Warsaw Pact. The lightweight Sting Ray anti-submarine torpedo costs a total of £900 millions for example, but this expenditure includes research, development, production and service for the finest light-weight torpedo in the world. The 'thinking torpedo', as it has been called, is certainly the only one with an overwhelming chance of detecting and sinking any type of enemy submarine.

The argument that I deployed to the doubters who queried this colossal expenditure was that it was no use having vastly expensive launching platforms (the Sting Ray is used from helicopters, maritime patrol Nimrods and surface ships) if they do not have a truly effective weapon to launch. Sting Ray, which entered service ahead of its planned date, to be used if necessary in the South

Atlantic Battle in April 1982, will now remain in service, with updating from time to time, for many years.

But all the money you need, and we certainly did not have that, is no substitute for skilled people with high morale and I think it fair to say that morale was rather brittle in the fleet in those early months of the new government. Although the pay review board's increase was fully implemented straight away I found, when I visited ships at sea a week or so later, a deep suspicion among junior ratings until they had actually seen the increased pay and had it in their pockets. Accordingly I made a priority of getting around the fleet and shore establishments to see and be seen and to talk informally and 'off the record' with the officers in the wardroom, the junior ratings in their messdecks and always with the Chiefs and Petty Officers in their messes.

Apart from pay there was genuine concern, never fully allayed over my two years, about the lack of critical spare parts for weapons and radar and electronic equipment. The sailor of today, as the Falklands has shown, is highly professional and he wants his ship to be a hundred per cent operational. It is frustrating and bad for morale if her effectiveness is being constantly eroded by shortcomings in spares caused by failings by the manufacturers or by naval stores or, alas, all too often by some cash crisis of government.

At the same time these visits showed me that the modern sailor has a better respect for and understanding of the Soviet naval threat than his civilian counterpart or indeed most politicians. This is not surprising since elements of the Soviet fleet are uninvited participants at most major NATO naval exercises and their submarines and aircraft are frequent 'camp followers'.

I found these visits invaluable and for the two years I was Minister I spent about a third of my time out of the office and seeing the ships, the commandos, the dockyards and the training establishments. Having been in the Navy and Naval Reserve for so long I always felt at home and knew the language which was a great help. Every profession today gets more and more technical and every profession has its own jargon—the Navy's is particularly colourful, much based on tradition. It just saved a great deal of time if you knew what people were talking or writing about and the difference between, for example, sonar, sosus, and a sono-buoy. (Three different sound systems for detecting submarines.)

The Navy is really one large family. I have found this true in the

United States and Netherlands too. This means that when you serve in a ship you almost invariably know at least one other person aboard and often you have served before with large numbers. So it was that I, as Minister, was continually bumping into old friends. In the Ministry, at sea, as Naval attachés abroad, faces and friends from the past would reappear, and old ties be renewed. For most of my time the Navy's Director of Public Relations was Captain Tony Collins who was my House Cadet Captain thirty years before at Dartmouth. Another House Cadet Captain and old friend was Captain Jeremy Black who worked with me in the Ministry and then went to command *Invincible* and do a marvellous job in the South Atlantic Conflict. Captain David Pentreath, another friend from cadet days, left the Ministry to command HMS *Plymouth* and had a remarkable battle in the Falklands and received the surrender of South Georgia in his cabin. There are many more I could mention but the point is that at a significant level in the Navy I had a considerable number of old friends whom I respected and trusted. I like to think they had similar feelings for their Minister.

I relived part of this past when I went in my official capacity to the Royal Naval College Dartmouth where I had served as a cadet from 1947-1951. To my surprise and delight there were still one or two masters and instructors there whom I remembered from all those years ago. They were kind enough to say that they remembered me which is a nice thought!

Dartmouth now also trains the special duties officer candidates who are those who hope to be commissioned having advanced through the ranks, together with the WRNS Officer cadets, and is a much cosier place than the somewhat spartan regime thought appropriate for the thirteen years old cadets who were its mainstay for generations. I freely admit I enjoyed going back as a VIP staying in the Captain's house and gazing at the dormitory where my bed used to be all those years ago. Captain Nick Hunt with whom I was staying had dug out my old term photograph and it was in pride of place in my bedroom that evening. I positively wallowed in nostalgia.

It was at Dartmouth that I wore my 'Admiralty Board Uniform' for the first time. Naval regulations prescribe a special Navy reefer jacket with Admiralty buttons, white shirt, Admiralty Board tie, Navy trousers and white cap with Admiralty Board badge that may be worn by civilian members of the Admiralty Board when on duty.

The last person, I believe, to wear this was Lord Carrington when he was First Lord of the Admiralty in the early 1960s. I believed it was a good idea for two reasons. Firstly you could properly return salutes and other marks of respect paid to you as Navy Minister. Secondly at a ship or shore establishment you were immediately identified and did not get confused with a private secretary or another civilian member of staff. With the help of Lieutenant Commander Patrick Suther, Flag Lieutenant to the Admiralty Board, and Felicity my first Wren P.A. we made the necessary arrangements.

Later we developed a 'woolly pully' version in navy blue for submarines, helicopters and other exotic forms of transport. Not to be outdone the Royal Marines designed a khaki 'woolly pully' version which I wore when visiting their units. I believe the whole concept worked well and the servicemen and women liked to see 'their Minister' being identified in what was really a very old tradition.

However, much work of a strategic nature had to be done in the Ministry, not least in planning the longer term fleet and its support facilities. There clearly were some deficiencies even in the existing ships. I was particularly concerned about the lack of a close-range weapons system in the 'Invincible' Class. Her only armament, apart from her aircraft, was her Sea Dart missile launcher on the fo'c'sle. This was a medium range weapon and not any good for close air or indeed sea attack. When this shortcoming was raised by the Conservative Member for Cambridge Robert Rhodes James in a parliamentary Navy Debate in June 1980 I replied in terms of sympathetic agreement. [13] The problem again was money but it seemed to me that a light-weight Sea Wolf close-range missile system would greatly improve the self-defence characteristics of these new carriers. I determined that this should be done as soon as the money and systems were available.

The other major problem was the future shape of the fleet. I found total realism among my Admiralty Board Colleagues that we just could not afford high-technology gold-plated solutions for every problem.

At the same time we could not discharge both our NATO and national responsibilities with a comparatively small number of very sophisticated ships. I believed and still believe the solution to this problem is to develop what historically, in one form or another, the Navy has always had, the concept of first and second rate frigates or ships of the line.

In other words different qualities and sizes of ships to back up one another with the second-rate vessels being cheaper to build, man and run.

In modern terms this meant the expensive but very capable Type 22 frigates with their helicopters, Sea Wolf and Exocet missiles and anti-submarine torpedoes could be supplemented by a much cheaper, smaller Type 23 frigate with a more limited range of weapons. Similarly the costly 'all singing all dancing' 'Hunt' Class Mine Counter Measures Ships would be supplemented by a new type of single-role mine hunter, less effective but half the price, which in turn would be supplemented by very cheap trawler-type mine-sweepers manned by the Royal Naval Reserve to deal with specific types of mines.

It is not stretching this whole idea too far to consider supplementing the sophisticated command and control facilities and flight deck of the 'Invincible' class carriers with a deck built on oil tankers or container ships so that additional Sea Harriers or helicopters can be operated. All these would be directed and under the control of the carrier and possibly have lift-on-board light-weight containerised weapon systems of the Sea Wolf or Sea Dart kind.

All this forward thinking and a realistic hard look at financial constraints led to various expensive projects for future air defence surface ships being abandoned. They would have been just too costly in terms of cash and manpower to run them. The additional overspending of the Ministry's sum allowed in 'cash-limits' led to some cuts or deferments in the programme in 1980 and the so-called moratorium on spare parts and equipment. The moratorium lasted for several months and we Ministers had to give personal approval for purchases or contracts above a certain value. It was time-consuming and frustrating. However it did encourage a 'self-help' rather than 'help-yourself' attitude and it did pinpoint waste and inefficiencies in the system. Francis Pym, the Secretary of State, publicly expressed his distaste for the cash limits system our Ministry had to work under, with its lack of flexibility unless some special deal was done with the Treasury. To try and home in at the end of the financial year with accuracy and precision on your spending target in a budget of what was then £12,000 millions was to say the least damned difficult. You were just as likely to underspend as overspend while much of your money on long-term capital projects like ships and aircraft was bespoken for several years ahead and could not be changed very much in any event. I believed that a rolling programme with a balance of expenditure against cash limits over say a three to four year period would have made much more sense.

One major problem which was always with us were Her Majesty's Royal Dockyards. These were sited at Devonport, Rosyth in Scotland, Portsmouth, Chatham and Gibraltar. In earlier years dockyards in places like Singapore, Malta and Sheerness had closed and in the United Kingdom some 32,000 workers were employed in the four yards plus nearly 2000 in Gibraltar. A modern ship is a very complex piece of machinery, It has to be serviced and maintained, modernised and repaired. Some of this work is done as a matter of routine by the ship's own staff perhaps with a certain amount of shoreside support. Much however has to be done by skilled craftsmen and technicians using the many facilities that only dockyards can provide.

The employees in the dockyards are for the most part industrial civil servants. They are bound by the rules and procedures of the civil service which appeared to me to be at best irrelevant to modern industrial life and at worst actively hostile to it. In 1979 pay was a problem, as in the Services, and dockyard workers with special skills were leaving in droves to go to better paid jobs in outside industry. A shortage of electricians, for instance, would mean that other workers would remain in paid idleness until the electricians had finished a job and they could move in. Productivity consequently was poor, efficiency low, morale not good, while the customer, the Navy, complained of lack of capacity, high costs and over-runs on the completion time of refits.

This was not, alas, a new problem. In 1950/1 the Select Committee on estimates in their 8th and 9th reports had dealt with dockyard problems. So had the estimates committee in its 9th report in 1962 and its 5th special report in 1963. Then a special committee under Sir John Mallabar produced a detailed report on dockyards and Royal Ordnance Factories in 1971. The response to all these reports was by and large to let them gather dust in the murky depths of the Ministry and tinker with the dockyard administration rather than tackling the structural reform that many believed was needed.

It was in October 1979 that Francis Pym asked me to chair a new study into 'the rôle, organisation and structure of the Royal Dockyards in the United Kingdom'. The study was asked to 'consider how the Royal Dockyards might best be organised to meet the requirements of the Royal Navy in the 1980s and 1990s'. I had a powerful team to assist me on the steering group including senior civil servants, naval officers and outside management consultants with a back-up working group of bright naval officers, members of the corps of naval constructors and civil servants.

Mightily we laboured and visited not once but several times each of the home dockyards. We had frank and very positive meetings with management and unions. We looked at the best practices among our allies. We took evidence from MPs, local authorities, naval officers and the general public. It was a very hard grind but, I felt, infinitely worthwhile because everyone we spoke to recognised there was a problem and was anxious to help try to solve it.

We finally produced the Report at the end of April 1980 and I was determined that we should not pull our punches. In chapter two of the report we spoke of 'A crisis in the dockyards'; we went on to say, 'the dockyards are failing to meet the increasing needs of the Royal Navy. Management recognises this but lacks authority to respond to the growing difficulties. The workforce is discontented about pay and fearful of the future ... The operational capability and morale of the Royal Navy has been put under particular strain and Fleet readiness has been affected.' All this plain speaking was, to say the least, unconventional for an official report.

Our solutions were radical but realistic. We put forward detailed suggestions to give dockyard managers more freedom to manage resources including earnings and manpower and in return be held accountable for each dockyard's performance against firm object-ives. Each would be treated as a separate 'profit centre' with its own trading fund. Comparison and competition should be developed between dockyards where possible and between the Royal Dock-yards and dockyards in the commercial sector.

In other words we should cut as many links as possible from the Civil Service attitude which was inappropriate for running a considerable industrial enterprise comparable in size to Vauxhall

Motors or The Metal Box Co. There were many other proposals most of which are standard practice in well run profitable organisations but were greatly daring in a dockyard Civil Service context.

The study rejected for the time being the injection of private capital into the dockyards. We also came out very firmly for the retention of all four home yards and believed, in fairness to the employees concerned, that an early decision should be made and announced about this. After the report had been considered by ministerial colleagues I was authorised on behalf of the government to accept these two recommendations and make a public announcement to this effect.

This was done by my answering a Parliamentary Question from Peggy Fenner the MP for Rochester and Chatham in August 1980, when I said, 'The Government accepts the recommendation in the report and confirms the need to retain the four home dockyards though the levels of employment in each dockyard will depend on the success of their management and workforce in improving efficiency. The Government also accepts the report's conclusion that the introduction of private capital into the dockyards is not a practical solution at this time ...' [14]

A consultative document based 99 per cent on the original study was then published, and together with my colleagues who produced the Report I went back on the dockyard trail discussing it with unions and management. The reaction was excellent from all concerned. I think because the Report was seen by all to be fair and objective, Management, Unions and the Navy swallowed those bits they did not like and offered genuine co-operation to get it off the ground. The Whitehall machine did not react with such clarity or decision however, and time started to elapse and I started to grow increasingly impatient.

The answer came on 25th June 1981, less than eleven months after the Government's commitment on keeping the four dockyards open. The Secretary of State for Defence in his White Paper 'The Way Forward' (Command 8288) announced the proposed closure of Chatham Dockyard and the dramatic running down of Portsmouth Dockyard to a fraction of its size. A few months later the closure of Gibraltar dockyard during 1983 was announced. The Speed Dockyard Study joins the others mouldering in those murky depths and a great opportunity to bring one part of our industrial civil service into the latter half of the twentieth century (and have it run along good Conservative principles too) has been lost. By this time of course I had been dismissed.

One part of my responsibilities that never lay and gathered dust was that relating to the Royal Marines. I never failed to be impressed by their smartness and dedicated professionalism, whether it was in their training camps in Britain or on their deployments out of the country. Every winter 45 and 42 Commandos spend three months Arctic training in Norway and in 1980 and 1981 I visited them and saw for myself what a very talented group they were to train themselves for fighting in the snow in sub-zero weather conditions. To survive in North Norway out of doors in mid-winter is no mean achievement, but to ski, march, fight, carry out amphibious landings, operate helicopters and the Volvo 'Bandwagon' snow vehicles all with great skill and elan was a heart-warming experience to watch. Their Arctic uniforms are white for camouflage and their weapons are taped white to help disguise them. A cheerful young black Marine from South London roared with laughter when we both had to agree that he had a camouflage problem. 'Perhaps,' he said, 'they'll think my face is a king-size fire cone!'

These young men with their Norwegian, Canadian, American and Dutch colleagues have a vital task to protect NATO's Northern flank, an area that I and many others think could be particularly vulnerable in any future conflict or time of tension. The North Norwegian air bases there are of critical importance for providing air cover over the Norwegian and Arctic seas and the eastern North Atlantic.

I found a similar positive spirit among the Royal Marines when I visited them in Northern Ireland. I decided that every time a Commando was sent there on security duty I would wish to have a day with them, as well as later seeing the Navy playing its part in Northern Ireland operations. These trips had to remain secret until after I had returned and it was always with a feeling of deceit that I misled my family and colleagues until safely back at RAF Northolt.

The accommodation for the Marines left much to be desired; the danger was always present and you could not afford to relax from your guard for a minute—yet the enemy was not obvious, nor distinctive, and that made it much worse. Most of the time I went from one unit to another by helicopter at high speed and low height. Marine briefings, attitudes and efficiency were always first class. Only once did I feel a real unease and that was when I drove out of the police/military compound in Crossmaglen, right on the border, in an armoured car. As we trundled down the main street and round the square I was aware of a feeling of incipient evil that ran shivers down my spine. True, British soldiers have died brutally there and this may have affected my perception. Whatever the reason it is not a place I would willingly wish to return to in a hurry; during my life I have finished up in some pretty rum places on occasions but no other had this effect before or since.

The financial squeeze continued through 1980 and, to my real and everlasting regret, as well as cuts in various programmes of all the services we found it necessary to disband 41 Commando and disperse the Officers and Marines to 40, 42 and 45 Commandos. This at least meant three reasonably strong units rather than four weaker ones, although the actual reorganisation did not take place until May 1981.

The pressures on both Francis Pym personally and the defence budget in the Autumn of 1980 were considerable, although we had already achieved a reduction of over 15,000 civil servants, a much more efficient use of men and materials and we had been obliged to postpone and delay various important defence orders. But defence inflation was exceeding normal inflation, we were having to pay the increased service salaries to make good the deficiencies that our predecessors had bequeathed us, and a lot of naval ship building was beginning to approach the expensive stage. It was a time of much hard work, budget trimming and not much light ahead.

The high point of that gloomy period was a day that belonged to two ladies. HMS *Leeds Castle*, the first of a new Class of off-shore patrol vessel, was to be launched by Peggy my wife on 22nd October. The ship was being built by the small but very capable firm of Hall Russell in Aberdeen. Peggy and I flew up the night before which was Trafalgar Night and we toasted 'The Immortal Memory' of Lord Nelson at a very pleasant dinner party given by the ship builders.

A launch is surrounded by nautical superstitions and if something goes wrong it can be very bad 'joss' and affect the ship all her life. Terrifying stories have been told of the lady 'sponsor' forgetting her lines, or the champagne bottle not breaking after repeated and hysterical swings at the bows. At some launches the ship, anxious to reach her natural environment, has slid gracefully down the slipway while the official party are still taking their places and the vessel has had to be pursued by a determined sponsor waving a bottle in a small boat. Other ships have defied all efforts by the shipwright to move at all until long after the ceremony is over and the guests departed.

So it was with some trepidation that the day dawned for Peggy and for Jimmy Milne, the genial new boss of Hall Russell. It was his first launch since he took over the responsibility and involved a brand new class of ship whose habits, stability and trim had been calculated but not tried in practice.

In the event it was a magnificent launching. The check umbrella thoughtfully provided by Hall Russell to protect us from the rain matched Peggy's suit. The Royal Marine band played with great gusto. The Service was moving and Peggy word perfect. The champagne bottle smashed most satisfactorily and a few seconds later *Leeds Castle* safely entered the water. At the lunch that followed my wife had to make a speech and I had to reply on behalf of the Admiralty Board, altogether a memorable day.

HMS *Leeds Castle* was commissioned into the Fleet a year later in October 1981 and then served with distinction in the Battle of the South Atlantic in 1982. My wife keeps a close liaison with 'her own ship', and I believe there could be a considerable future for this type of vessel both in the Royal Navy and for export to other navies.

The only other bright spot in what was left of 1980 was a most interesting and useful visit made to Diego Garcia and Hong Kong. Diego Garcia, about 1000 miles North Eastish of Mauritius, is part of the British Indian Ocean Territories and over the past ten or more years has been developed as a naval and air base by the Americans with up to 3000 personnel permanently stationed there. It is a horseshoe-shaped island nineteen miles from tip to toe with a large deepwater lagoon providing an excellent anchorage. At times the island is only a few yards wide and the uninhabited portion is populated by wild donkeys. This remote outpost of the British Empire is run by two Royal Naval Officers and twenty-six ratings assisted of course by the American security squads. They provide the justice, customs, post office and other facilities including a hard crackdown on drug offences among some of the Americans on the island.

Strangely enough I was the first British Minister ever to visit Diego Garcia and my arrival in an RAF VC10 accompanied by Margaret my private secretary and Lynda my Second Officer (Wrens) personal assistant caused a minor sensation. The film '100 Men and a Girl' was updated to '3000 men and two girls'. In fact the whole scene, palm trees and all, was reminiscent of 'South Pacific' and I expected the American Sailors and Marines to burst into 'There is nothing like a dame'!

The visit was extremely useful and I was most impressed by the senior US Navy Officers and their plans for the expansion of the facilities. We ironed out or 'identified' a number of problems on both the British and American sides which were to be tackled when we got home. We were popular with the 'Brits' because our plane had brought out all the traditional British Christmas 'goodies' and we were able to take back a lot of the heavy luggage of those who were being relieved. Being British and Navy they had their own club with their own British beer and we enjoyed a splendid evening playing darts and drinking beer under the tropical stars. When we left to go on to Hong Kong our people were very anxious we should depart with style.

I had a word with our genial and very competent RAF pilot who entered into the spirit of the thing. We departed on the Saturday morning and it seemed that all Diego Garcia had turned out to see us off in our VC10 jet, an unusual aeroplane for them.

We did a normal take-off, climbed to about 1000 feet, turned and flew back at right angles to the runway descending with the engines idling. When we got to 600 feet immediately over the runway the throttles were slammed to 95% power and we shot up like a rocket leaving the roar of four Rolls-Royce Conways in full cry behind us.

We got a laconic 'game, set and match' from the control tower and, I understand, left a pleasurable after-glow with the small but distinguished Royal Navy contingent on the island!

A danger of all this travelling and ministerial high jinks is that an 'Ivory Tower' complex can develop. Any Minister who neglects his constituents, Parliament and his fellow MPs does so at his peril. I used to take great care and pains over the answers to Parliamentary questions and the 'supplementaries' they generated. For some reason, and I always regarded it as a good sign, the Navy did not get as many questions as the other two services. I have always found in my political life that, on the whole, no news is good news. If people are reasonably content they don't write and they rarely ask questions. Defence Ministers have one advantage that they share with their Foreign Office colleagues and that is they usually have little legislation to steer through Parliament.

I spent and still spend a lot of time in the House of Commons, in the tearoom, the smoking room, the library and the lobbies, so that there was no danger of my getting divorced from Parliament. Often someone would have a point or a query which we could discuss personally then and there, and this made life easier for all concerned.

A minister often feels an imperative to work especially hard at and attend functions in his constituency. As far as Ashford was concerned I found great understanding and support in my work from my constituents even on those very few but inevitable occasions when I had to cancel a function at short notice because of some overriding ministerial commitment.

On 5th January 1981 I returned to my office after the New Year break. My staff had decided we would celebrate the return to work by having an evening party, and their expert culinary skills together with a lethal punch was much in evidence when my wife and I turned up just before it was due to start at six. Instead of sweetness and light the air was heavy and thick with apprehension and unspoken fears. It had the appearance of a requiem rather than a party.

Francis Pym's private secretary took me on one side. 'There has been a reshuffle—Francis Pym is to be the new Leader of the House and Mr Heyhoe (Army Minister) is to be promoted and go to the Civil Service Department.' I was dumbfounded.

'Who is to be the new Secretary of State?'

'Mr Nott.'

'I see.'

'Am I still the Navy Minister?' I asked.

'Yes, you and Mr Pattie have not been affected in any way.'

'In that case let's get on with the party,' I replied.

It was the last truly enjoyable occasion I was to have in the Ministry, and for both the Royal Navy and my own ministerial career the outlook would soon be stormy.

1 Admiral of the Fleet Sergei Gorshkov – creator of the largest navy the world has ever seen.

2 Returning from *Nimitz* in the C.O.D. after the catapult launch!

3   Inspecting an American guard of honour
with Graham Claytor, US Deputy
Secretary of Defense in Washington.

4   One way of getting from HMS *Lowestoft* to
HMS *Amazon*!

5 At the periscope of the Trident Submarine
USS *Daniel Boone*.

6 HMS *Invincible* with two Sea Harriers (note
her pennant number RO5!)

7 In the prototype AV8B with McDonnell
Douglas's "Jackie" Jackson.

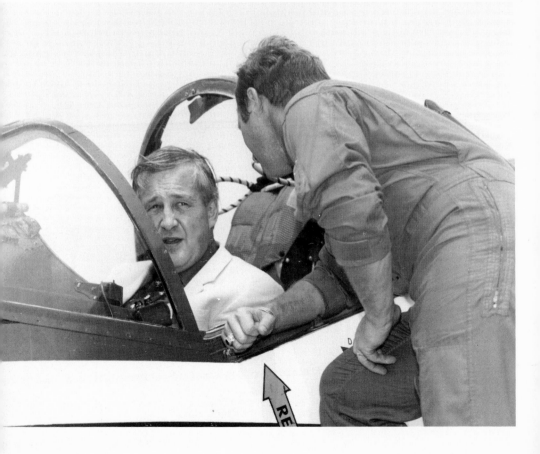

9   HMS *Endurance* watches over the damaged
Argentinian submarine *Santa Fe* towed by
two British tugs off South Georgia.

HMS *Leeds Castle*, the corvette of the
future.

10 20th August, 1982: *Endurance* returns to Chatham after eleven months in the South Atlantic.

7.   Nott Cuts and Speed Goes

At the start of 1981 the Ministry of Defence received not only a new Secretary of State, John Nott, but two other new Ministers as well: Lord Trenchard came from the Department of Industry to replace Lord Strathcona, who returned to the Lords back benches; and Philip Goodhart, who had been Parliamentary Under-Secretary in Northern Ireland, took over Barney Heyhoe's job as Army Minister. As I wryly remarked to Geoffrey Pattie, the Air Force Minister: 'We should both be fireproof for three months as we are the continuity men!' There was considerable speculation in the press that John Nott had been put into Defence to do a hatchet man's job that Francis Pym was not prepared to countenance. A few nights after his appointment, I was told by a very senior diplomat from a friendly NATO ally that this was certainly so.

In fact we were still grappling with the defence cuts of 1980 and it fell to John Nott to announce these on 20th January in Parliament. The Naval cuts included the merger of one of the Royal Marine Commandos (No 41) with the remaining three, the deferral of ship ordering, the closure of communication air squadrons and, six months earlier than was scheduled, the disposal of HMS *Bulwark*. The main naval programme remained more or less intact but we were living increasingly on a knife edge. I was becoming very bothered indeed about the delay in ordering new surface ships needed to maintain force numbers in the late 1980s and beyond. British shipbuilders particularly wanted more orders for Type 22 frigates and this was widely reported. I was getting very concerned too about the new trawler type minesweeper that we had promised the Royal Naval Reserve. Eventually there would be one for each of the twelve RNR Divisions and the first four should have been ordered in 1980. Since all twelve Minesweepers (Medium), as they were called, would cost less than a third of a Type 22 frigate I did not think this first order would exactly break the Ministry's bank. At one stage that January I thought that the ship building arguments had been accepted and some limited orders would be allowed, but it was not to be.

The existence within the Ministry at that time of three single-service Ministers did not give them the power to order main equipment. This was done by the Minister of State, for procurement in concert, on the major items, with the Secretary of State. If the Secretary of State and the central staffs who determined the service budgets exerted a squeeze on the cash available this effectively ruled out the question of new orders even before they were requested. There was usually money for ongoing contracts, which could take years to complete, but there was nothing in reserve for new ones. Indeed sometimes if the money looked like running out the cancellation or delaying of an existing contract was a serious possibility. Often only the threat of huge damages payments for a cancelled contract would stop such drastic steps being taken.

The next few weeks through February, March and April were the most frustrating and distasteful of my entire political life since I joined the Conservative Party in 1949, at the tender age of fifteen. They were punctuated by only a few incidents which lessened the general gloom and enabled me to keep a sense of perspective. One of these was the visit in March which I have already described to John Lehman and the Vice President of the United States. Another was my trip to inspect the Royal Marines in Norway where I saw 42 Commando engaged in their Arctic training. I vowed once again that if I am ever in a really tough spot I would rather have a Royal Marine Commando with me than anyone else.

I travelled on the flight deck of an RAF Hercules with General Robin Pringle, soon to become Commandant General Royal Marines and, later that year, to be badly injured in an IRA car bomb attack.

Fortunately his courage, strength and quiet good humour have led to a remarkable recovery. Though he lost a leg he was back at duty in the spring of 1982. We took it in turns to fly what is really quite a large aircraft to Trondheim in North Norway and on the way reported a tanker which was illegally discharging oil into the Norwegian Sea. I have it on good authority that not one of the sleeping troops in the back of the plane stirred whilst Robin and I were at the controls!

Other high spots included a visit to Chatham at the end of

January for the commissioning ceremony, after a major refit, of the Type 12 frigate HMS *Plymouth*. Her Commanding Officer, Captain David Pentreath, an old friend from cadet days, was the Captain in command of the Sixth Frigate Squadron. *Plymouth* was to distinguish herself in the Falklands Battle, but we were to meet again before that campaign. I also had an interesting and exciting day, together with the Chief Constable of Norfolk, aboard the *Indefatigable*, a gas rig off the Norfolk coast. We watched an exercise in which the rig had been taken over by 'terrorists' and was recaptured by special unit Royal Marines in a seaborne and helicopter assault. There is a special highly mobile Royal Marine Unit called Commacchio Company, several hundred strong, based at Arbroath in Scotland and trained to do this and other special security work. The Company was formed in May 1980 and its members are drawn from all the various commandos. We had no sooner arrived aboard the rig for the pre-exercise briefing than alarm bells started ringing and lights flashing a fire warning. A fire aboard a gas rig is not my idea of a good afternoon's entertainment. Fortunately it was a false alarm, the first they had experienced for many months.

However, as the weeks went by it was clear we were in for a major defence review. The Healey Review had taken over twelve months and, as we have already seen, had involved many cabinet committee meetings. John Nott's was to take about twelve weeks and I doubt whether many meetings of the cabinet or its committees were involved. The Service budgets were, and as far as I know still are, worked out up to nine years ahead, in a long term costing programme designed to take into account the protracted completion time of capital projects, be they ships, aircraft, buildings or other major items. Each service has a proportion or target heading of the whole defence budget. The defence budget overall may increase in line with 'defence inflation', ordinary inflation, or not at all. This last case would of course mean a substantial cut in terms of what the money would buy. The programmes that deal with ships, manpower, weapons, equipment and support facilities all have to be worked out within these costings.

As has become clear since the spring of 1982 a number of alternatives for the future defence budgets were put forward and the different services were allocated, over a nine year period, different shares of that budget. The idea was to save money in total, but how savings were to be made would vary considerably for each service. The end result is that while in 1982 the Navy accounted for about twenty-nine per cent of Britain's defence budget, by the end of the 1980s it will be down to twenty-five per cent or even less, as has been admitted in Parliament.

In 1982 these four percentage points represented just under £600 millions or the equivalent of the cost of two 'Invincible' Class carriers a year. In global terms the 1981 defence review cut several thousand million pounds off the naval programme for the nine years to end in 1990. In addition the Navy was saddled with virtually the entire bill for the Trident submarine and missile programme. In the early 1960s, when the Polaris missiles and submarines were being acquired, the cost was designed to fall on the defence budget as a whole, rather than to be at the sole expense of one service.

From March 1982 onwards the general outline of the reduced future programme which could be funded became clear. The Admiralty Board and other Service Boards then struggled against the clock to adopt and reduce their programmes to meet new financial targets, subject to over-riding directives from the Secretary of State and the Government. As the First Sea Lord, Admiral Sir Henry Leach, said in his Royal United Service Institute Lecture on 9th June 1982: 'The informed recognise that it (last year's defence review) was done in a hurry, involved pre-judgment, and was driven by short term politico-economic expediency rather than long term strategic sense. The effect on the oyal Navy was dramatic....' The sort of strain that it imposed on Board Members and their staffs can be imagined, with meetings lasting until late at night, punctuated only by my dashing away when the division bell went for some vote in the Commons lobbies.

I do not know how these financial decisions and air, military and naval force directives were arrived at. Even if I did my lips would be sealed. But my belief is that the Defence Secretary, under a remit to contain the defence budget (and indeed save considerable sums over the decade from 1980), had convinced himself that the main Soviet submarine threat in the North Atlantic was best dealt with by more Nimrod Maritime Patrol Aircraft and by the maintainance of the Navy's hunter-killer submarine programme, albeit at a lower level. He, like Mr Healey before him, was not impressed by arguments for the Fleet to have its own organic air power; nor, like

102

Mr Healey, did he attach much importance to the Royal Navy's national as opposed to NATO duties. I may be doing John Nott an injustice but he certainly always took the view that 'weapons' were more important than 'platforms' and I know from press reports that he was scornful of my 'more hulls in the water' philosophy. I do not believe that he understood that the two could not be divorced. It is no good possessing, for instance, a very advanced light-weight Stingray anti-submarine torpedo which has cost hundreds of millions of pounds to develop, unless you have the helicopter, the flight deck, the maintenance, the hangar, the sonar and all the back-up of the ship to see that the torpedo is launched against the right target, in the right place at the right time. Anyway, all this is to an extent speculation. I was certainly not consulted in any detail about these important matters and the key outline of the review was settled within a few weeks.

It is difficult adequately to describe the sense of anger, frustration and growing disillusionment that I felt during April and early May 1981. I was Navy Minister in a Conservative Government headed by a Prime Minister whom I liked and respected, and appointed to strengthen the Navy. My own election address to my constituents in Ashford promised to 'make up deficiencies in our contribution to NATO, step up Naval and aircraft building and spares programmes and boost morale to stop skilled officers and NCOs leaving the services in large numbers'. Yet here I was feverishly working on plans to weaken the Navy and Royal Marines, to cut the surface fleet and its essential support and to make large numbers of Navy Officers and Ratings redundant. Since we had come into office the Soviet Fleet had continued its expansion in quality and quantity, as I have already shown, and Soviet Forces had invaded and occupied Afghanistan. Iran was fighting Iraq in a Middle East War that could jeopardise much of the West's oil. International terrorism was everywhere on the increase. In Poland there were continuous rumblings of rebellion from 'Solidarity'. All in all it seemed a crazy time to run down any forces, certainly to run down the Royal Navy and Royal Marines on the scale envisaged. I recalled my early days in the Ministry, going round the Fleet and the establishments, pledging a stronger Navy under new management and rebuilding morale and trust which are such important factors in the armed services.

On Tuesday 12th May I gave a lunch for an interesting party of Icelandic MPs, some of whom were clearly destined to become political leaders of their country in due course. I tried not to show the strain I was feeling, although that afternoon, in a strongly worded Minute, I made clear my profound disagreement with the course upon which we were headed. The next day, Wednesday 13th May, I hosted an Admiralty Board Dinner in Admiralty House for Admiral Sir Richard Clayton, the Commander-in-Chief Naval Home Command, to celebrate his forthcoming retirement. Dick Clayton shared my enthusiasm for motorcycling and had worked closely with me, being responsible for most naval shore training establishments and the Royal Naval Reserve. As one of the principal Commanders-in-Chief he was well aware of the grave problems we were facing and the critical battles being fought. Nevertheless it was an agreeable occasion, except that both my wife and I had a strong conviction it would be the last time we would act as hosts on an Admiralty Board occasion.

The following week, on Tuesday 19th and Wednesday 20th May, we were due to have a debate in Parliament on the 1981 Defence White Paper and estimates. The intention was that this would be a reasonably low-key affair and speculation or information about cuts of any kind were to be discouraged. In an introduction to the White Paper dated April 1981, the Defence Secretary had said: 'We must re-establish in the long term programme the right balance between the inevitable resource constraints and our necessary defence requirements. We need, therefore, to look realistically, and with an open mind, at the way in which our forces fulfil their rôles. I shall be considering in the coming months with the Chiefs of Staff, and in consultation with our allies, how technological and other changes can help us fulfil the same basic rôles more effectively in the future without the massive increase in real defence expenditure which the escalation of equipment costs might otherwise seem to imply.' [15]

This was probably how John Nott saw his Defence Review. It is certainly a philosophy that on the surface one could not quarrel with. Whether the end result accorded with this philosophy was, of course, another matter. Anyway this particular paragraph plus various leaks, hints and rumours alerted some of the brighter Fleet Street journalists to the fact that pretty fundamental changes were being considered. For a number of weeks speculative paragraphs had appeared about possible Naval and Royal Marine cuts and the tempo was warming up before the debate. I found myself in an increasingly impossible situation on two counts. Firstly, the whole budget and cuts operation was fast becoming 'set in concrete' and once it had been approved, even in outline, by key Ministers, it would be too late to change. Secondly, I did not believe we could get through two days of defence debating without some probing and penetrating questions from my Parliamentary colleagues on both the Conservative and Labour backbenches. Since I was 'winding up' the debates at the end of one of the days I had no intention of lying and saying there were not major cuts planned. Equally, it would have been virtually impossible to have covered the subject with a verbal smokescreen which might well have made matters worse. To be fair, this latter apprehension was not, I think, shared by many people in the Ministry. The Ministry felt we could have a humdrum sort of debate and the Defence Review White Paper could then follow in due course, when Parliament was near the summer recess. This was to start earlier than usual because of the wedding of the Prince and Princess of Wales at the end of July.

My arguments against the substance and form of the cuts having fallen on deaf ears, I then decided that, as Minister charged with responsibility for the Royal Navy, I had to make very clear how I saw those responsibilities being discharged. This was particularly important in view of the threat, as I perceived it, from my regular intelligence briefings. For several weekends past I had been working on a draft of a key speech which was designed to bring home to the general public the rôle and importance of the Royal Navy. This stressed the unique flexibility of maritime power, properly exercised, and the twin tasks of co-operating with our allies in NATO and working by ourselves for our national interests. I chose the words in the speech with great care since I did not wish publicly to criticise any colleague and I stressed on several occasions the vital need to get value for money.

However, I knew that my arguments for the Royal Navy and a balanced force of maritime patrol aircraft, helicopters, surface ships and submarines in adequate numbers, was a powerful one. I also knew that many of these arguments had been rejected by John Nott, as has since become abundantly clear. Yet I was the only politician with the necessary detailed knowledge to make the speech and advance the case. Civil servants and serving officers were not allowed to. In a sense I was making a speech that my Party had made many times in Opposition, when the Labour Government had been cutting the Fleet. I was also making a speech to warn against the irreversible running down of the Royal Navy and to explain the damage that could be caused to this country if this were to happen. I quoted Gorshkov's aims and philosophies, I listed the Soviet Fleet's strength and I reminded my fellow countrymen of our dependence on the sea for our trade: ninety-six per cent of our imports and exports travel by sea. I listed a whole series of non-NATO national tasks which I considered essential for the Royal Navy and Royal Marines including 'In the Antarctic.... showing a welcome presence to the Falkland Islanders'. Finally, I made it clear it was not more money for the Navy I was seeking, merely the maintaining of its current strength.

My wife typed the speech verbatim. It ran to over five foolscap pages and on Thursday 14th May I posted copies to the various specialist defence correspondents of the press and broadcasting companies. On it was a release time on the Friday evening when I was due to give the speech at Tenterden. Wild stories were subsequently spread by someone, I know not whom, that I had a special press lobby briefing meeting on the morning of Friday 15th May at which I gave all the confidential background information to the newsmen there gathered about the true nature and extent of the Navy cuts. This was rubbish. I had a normal morning in the office, a working lunch with a British Rail Manager to talk about consti- tuency matters and then went straight off to my constituency. Although my Ministry staff knew that I had prepared an important speech I did not show it to any of them, because if there were to be repercussions, I did not wish them to be hit by flying shrapnel! In addition, the speech was a political one being given at a political meeting and the rules were quite clear that the Ministry could not, rightly, be involved in such matters.

Thus it was on that Friday evening that I and sixty loyal members of the Tenterden Conservative Association, together with Arthur Hollis, my constituency Chairman, a shrewd genial ex-Lancaster pilot, and Robin Coombs, my agent, worked our way through the various items of business essential at the Annual General Meeting of any voluntary organisation in England. Finally, Gillian Mills, the Branch Chairman, gave me a generous introduction and I delivered my speech. It was well received, as were my answers to the questions that followed. The heavens did not fall in, no one present felt that they were participating in some new and meaningful experience or hearing a revolutionary doctrine of defence policy being propounded. I closely questioned a number of people, including Arthur Hollis, who is an old and valued friend, and their unanimous reaction was, 'Just the sort of speech we expect a Conservative Navy Minister to make'.

This was not quite the view of the BBC who tracked me down and did an interview on the 10 p.m. News Programme. They realised something was in the wind and tried hard to get me to say what Navy cuts were coming, but I refused to be drawn by them and the deluge of pressmen who followed. 'If there are to be major cuts these would be dangerous for the reasons I gave in my speech' was my line and I refused also to be critical of my colleagues. On the Saturday morning I opened a 'Help the Aged' Shop in Ashford, both a thoroughly worthwhile project and a happy escape for me, a couple of hours away from the telephone and the media.

Press interest continued unabated and Sunday's newspapers dealt at length with my speech and speculated about the cuts. Some of the speculation was quite well informed. I attended the Mayor of Tenterden's Civic Service, followed by a reception where perhaps one hundred and fifty constituents were present. I was warmed and heartened by the support and understanding of those I represented. Very few were defence experts but I have often found, on many important political matters, that the 'gut feeling' of the man in the street is more valuable than the opinions of all the experts lumped together.

I travelled up to London with Peggy by train on the Monday morning and carried on business as usual. John Nott and I had a meeting at noon, where we stated our positions! However, throughout this whole episode we remained civilised one to another and nobody banged desks or slammed doors. I'm sure that John regarded me as a king-size pain, just as I could not accept his policies as being in the national interest, but life is too short not to observe the proper courtesies.

A bizarre element now enters the story. When, some weeks previously, I had looked round the local telephone exchange the Manager had suggested I might care to have a post office 'bleeper' for trial purposes, to see if it would help a busy Minister. My personal assistant, if she wished to get in touch with me urgently, would dial a certain number, the bleeper in my pocket would 'bleep' and I would know to ring her as soon as possible. This gadget duly arrived and I carried it for the first time that Monday.

In the evening, with Peggy, my wife, I drove out to the Chinese Defence Attaché's house in St John's Wood, North London, where we had been invited for dinner. There we were joined by one of his colleagues from the embassy, making a friendly party of five around the table. The Peking-style food was excellent and I was just starting the second course when the bleeper went. I rang Lynda, my Personal Assistant, who was more than a little bothered and put me through directly to the Secretary of State. He was polite but to the point: Would I submit my resignation? I was equally polite and to the point: I declined to do so. In which case would I please telephone Number 10, Downing Street? The request was repeated there. I replied that I did not consider I had done anything that merited resignation, but if the Prime Minister wished to dismiss me that, of course, was her prerogative. It was accordingly arranged that I would see the Prime Minister in her room in the Commons at ten o'clock and I returned to finish my excellent Chinese dinner. I had no desire to disturb my hosts or my wife, so I said there was an unexpected vote and I had to be back at the House by 10 p.m. and Peggy could follow later.

Accordingly I left the dinner party early. The Prime Minister and I had a courteous and civilised forty-five minute interview, though one that was not particularly easy for either of us. She stuck to her guns, I stuck to mine. Just before midnight I was no longer Navy Minister, having agreed a form of words that made it clear that I was dismissed and did not resign. Both Peggy and Steve my driver were shattered; I was suprisingly calm. I had known subconsciously, for a long time, that there was no way I could implement the new policy with which I profoundly disagreed. At least my conscience was clear: I had done my best to change the policy and failed. The chances were there would at least now be a public debate about defence and our maritime rôle.

I went into the office on Tuesday morning, 19th May, to clear my desk and say my farewells. It was a great wrench leaving my private office staff who had served me so well. The Navy, the Royal

Marines, the Civil Servants were all very kind and I realised how privileged I had been to work with such people for two years. After saying my farewells to the First Sea Lord, Second Sea Lord and Chief of Fleet Support I left First's room to go down the corridor to the lift and to travel the six floors down to ground level.

To my utter astonishment the corridors and lobby were full of waving, cheering Naval and Royal Marine Officers who worked in the Ministry. Accompanied by the First Sea Lord I made my way, seeing them but dimly, into the lift. I was greatly moved at what was a marvellous demonstration of friendship and understanding. Henry Leach saw me into the car and Steve drove me for the last time down Whitehall. We were both too choked to speak but I managed to croak out my thanks on arrival at the Commons. I was sure we would not lose touch, and so it has proved.

That afternoon, after giving more press interviews, including one to my local newspaper the *Kentish Express*, whose editor had come up to London especially, I made my first ever speech as a back-bencher in government. Instead of winding up the debate as Minister I spoke from the traditional bench below the gangway seat reserved for recently departed Ministers. I told the House: 'I was not elected by my constituents nor appointed by my Right Honourable Friend the Prime Minister to preside over any major cutback in the surface fleet of the Royal Navy.' I went on to 'express to the House my profound unease that decisions could be taken which would have a damaging and lasting effect upon the fleet and its support'. [16]

The Defence Secretary opened the debate on the Tuesday and closed it on the Wednesday. He said, fairly, that final decisions had not yet been taken. In his speech was the implication that I was making a mountain out of a molehill. He was pretty dismissive of Admiral Gorshkov, whom I had quoted, and he was very sharp indeed about some national defence correspondents who had been making forecasts of possible Navy cuts, forecasts that events were to prove remarkably near the mark. In parliamentary terms it was judged to be a very good performance. While I had much sympathy, kindness and understanding from parliamentary colleagues and some of the press, I believe that there were many who thought that naval cuts of the magnitude speculated in some papers were just impossible and that somehow I had got it wrong....

The next few weeks saw my postbag contribute to the Post Office's record profit! Letters came in by the hundreds from all over the country and indeed from all over the world. People wrote to me from the USA, Saudi Arabia, Australia, Italy, Germany and Norway. I received about 2000 letters at that time on the subject of the Royal Navy and I can recall only three against my stand. Leading politicians of Labour and Liberal Parties wrote privately to me in support. The constituency people were magnificent, the local papers gave me good and fair coverage.

My local Conservative Association held an emergency meeting of their Executive Council on Friday 22nd May when over 120 people turned up. I gave a low key speech for twenty minutes or so, answered questions for half an hour and got unanimous backing and a standing ovation as Peggy and I left. I describe these events with no sense of arrogance or righteousness but to underline the deep conviction I have that there is much wisdom in the British people and when the going gets rough you find out who your true friends are. This support from my 'home base' was to fortify and strengthen me in the long and difficult months ahead.

At the end of June 1981 the results of the defence review which had been started three months earlier were published in the White Paper, 'Defence, the Way Forward'. [17] This document was like an ageing striptease star, more interesting for what it concealed than what it revealed. However, in its pages and in the debate that followed on the 7th July, the full extent of the Navy cuts started to become apparent. I say started because other decisions were to dribble out before the year end to complete the overall picture.

The total result of all this was that the number of anti-submarine warfare carriers was to be reduced by a third as was their Sea Harrier capability. This meant that the carrier *Hermes* would be disposed of when *Illustrious* became operational and *Invincible* would go when *Ark Royal* joined the Fleet. There was then to be some rejigging. It was proposed to sell *Invincible* to Australia at the bargain basement price of £175 millions. As she was only eighteen months old and would cost over £300 millions to replace, this seemed a pretty crazy form of stripping the Navy's assets. *Hermes* then would stay on with *Illustrious* until the *Ark Royal* was ready. The effect of reducing the number of our operational carriers by one third from three to two meant that the Navy could never guarantee

110

to have two operational together. Refitting, repairs, maintenance, accidents even, meant that, even with three, we could only guarantee the availability of one carrier at any given time. With three, however, there was always a pretty good chance that two would be ready for duties at any one time.

Having slashed the carrier force, the next proposals were that the amphibious floating dock assault ships *Intrepid* and *Fearless* should be prematurely scrapped. *Intrepid* was to go in 1982 and *Fearless* a couple of years later. This effectively deprived the Royal Marines of their main amphibious assault force, as these ships could mount an assault by landing craft or helicopter or both.

Continuing the cuts in the Navy, the destroyer/frigate force was to be reduced over three or four years from sixty-five to forty-two operational ships plus eight in reserve at long notice for availability. This was to be achieved by a combination of selling or scrapping existing destroyers of the County and Type 82 Classes and frigates of the Leander, Type 12 and Type 81 Classes. In practical terms, the number of truly operational escort ships would probably be in the low thirties since, inevitably, a number of them would be having essential refits and maintenance and not immediately available for sea service. At the same time new orders for frigates and mine-sweepers were sharply curtailed.

HMS *Endurance*, the Antarctic patrol and survey ship which had many years of good life ahead of her and was an essential link with the Falklands and South Georgia, was to be paid off and sold or scrapped after her patrol in the South Atlantic ended in the spring of 1982. I believe that this decision was to contribute to the key events leading up to the South Atlantic conflict. Her premature retirement was intended to save the Ministry of Defence nearly £3 millions a year!

Originally, twenty hunter-killer nuclear powered submarines had been planned for the Fleet. This figure then came down to seventeen, with the early scrapping of *Dreadnought*. However, as I have already mentioned, eighteen have to be built to achieve even this reduced target. A number of Royal Fleet Auxiliary tankers or stores ships were to be prematurely disposed of, to keep pace with the surface fleet reductions. The hovercraft trials unit at Lee on Solent was finally disbanded in spring 1982 and the Royal Navy's one jetfoil HMS *Speedy* did not complete her operational evaluation but was paid off in April 1982 and put up for sale, thus withdrawing the RN from a valuable new area of maritime tactics and technology. (This ship was not named after me; there have been 'Speedys' in the Navy since the 18th century!)

In terms of manpower, the aim was to reduce the Royal Navy by 10,000 Officers and Ratings in the five years up to 1986, with further reductions of a similar order in the remainder of the decade. A parallel reduction in the number of civilians giving back-up support was also to be made. The Royal Navy that remained would be the smallest for well over one hundred years.

To achieve more major financial savings the dockyard and naval base at Chatham was to be closed in 1983, while that at Portsmouth was to be drastically run down to a fleet maintenance base. Many shore establishments used for training, stores and back-up support were to be closed. And in the autumn it was announced that Gibraltar dockyard was to share Chatham's fate and be totally shut down, with a loss in the colony of some 1900 jobs out of a total population of under 30,000. The gross financial savings to the Ministry of Defence by these dockyard closures is estimated to amount to £140 millions a year by 1985, split £65 millions each for Chatham and Portsmouth and £10 millions for Gibraltar. The net savings to the United Kingdom, after closing-down costs, redundancy payments, resettlement grants, special aid for Gibraltar, and continuing unemployment pay for those displaced who cannot find work, are clearly very much less. Total job losses would probably be 13,000 men and women at these three yards.

However, much of this comes out of pockets other than the Defence Ministry's, including Social Security, Employment and Overseas Aid, so the Navy loses major and much needed facilities, the taxpayer is not much better off, but the Ministry of Defence can show a substantial saving in its budget. In industry this way of doing things is called 'a lack of corporate approach'.

Running down the dockyards means that, as a deliberate act of policy, mid-life modernisation of a ship's weapon systems, radar and sonar sets and all its electronic equipment just cannot take place. To give an example, HMS *York*, the last Type 42 destroyer to be built, will enter service in the autumn of 1984. She will still be in service well into the first years of the next century, yet under the new 'no modernisation' policy she will be equipped with weapon and radar systems designed to meet the threat of the 1970s and '80s. I cannot believe that a potential enemy is going to be considerate enough to allow his ships to become obsolete, so that he does not have an unfair advantage over us.

With the closure of these three dockyards it is clear not only that we are foregoing the capacity to modernise and enhance ships and their equipment but that we are also losing capacity and flexibility in specialist ship repair and preparation for war or emergencies. The need for this was highlighted in all five dockyards during and after the Falklands operation.

The closure of Chatham has even more disturbing implications, since it is the only dockyard in the country that has a good track record of successfully refitting and refuelling a whole stream of hunter-killer nuclear-powered submarines. To close this facility down and transfer all the work to Devonport which, in the Autumn of 1982, had still to complete one successful SSN refit, is not only putting all your eggs in one basket but I believe placing in jeopardy the whole of our hunter-killer programme. I am certain that prevarication over the future of *Dreadnought*, the Royal Navy's first nuclear powered hunter-killer submarine, was because of capacity problems that were building up with the decision to close Chatham. That is why the problem was finally solved by scrapping her. Yet a *Dreadnought* replacement, at £190 millions, will eat up three years' alleged gross savings due to accrue when Chatham closes and many years more of the real or net savings.

There were to be other casualties as the true effects of the cuts were revealed. Planned improvements to the medium range surface-to-air missile system Sea Dart, to correct its known shortcomings, were cancelled. Much needed replacements for the ageing hydrographic fleet were not to proceed and the Fast Training Boat Squadron was scrapped and naval exercises curtailed. Although not all of this was to be immediately understood by many people, the debate in July was a pretty pro-naval affair and, in the vote to approve the White Paper, a number of Conservative backbenchers joined me in refusing to vote with the Government.

Three days after this debate, on Friday 10th July, Lord Carrington, then Foreign Secretary, was due to come to my constituency and speak at a meeting, organised for me by my constituency Conservative Women's Committee. The venue was Tenterden, scene of the speech which had resulted in my sacking. Peter Carrington had been in Moscow most of the week, engaged in gruelling talks with his Russian counterparts. He had, therefore, a very genuine excuse to cry off, since he was very tired. It is typical of him that, not only did he come and 'do his stuff' superbly well, but he was kind enough to say some very nice things about me to my constituents. I was deeply saddened when he joined the 'ex-Ministers' Club' some eight months later.

My departure from the Ministry left a gap and for a couple of weeks there was no appointment. Then came the startling news that the posts of Navy, Army and Airforce Ministers were to be abolished. In future, under the Secretary of State, there would be a Minister of State and a Parliamentary Secretary for the Armed Forces. Thus, at a stroke, the problem of finding a replacement was solved and the danger that a Minister would be tempted to defend a particular service against the Treasury's depredations was removed. This decision also concentrated more power in the hands of the Secretary of State and the Chief of Defence Staff and thus ensured a more centralised approach, a marked contrast to the direction of defence political management in the United States.

I believe this to be an entirely wrong decision, for a number of reasons. Firstly, no one nowadays, and this is no criticism of individual people, can be sufficiently expert about the Army, Airforce, Navy, Marines and their auxiliary and support services. Increasingly, Ministers will have to rely on the service 'experts', either uniformed or civil service, and this is wrong. Secondly, the services like to feel that they have a recognisable political head who is there to see fair play on their behalf. British servicemen have always relied upon their uniformed and political chiefs to look after their interests and have always rejected the practice of a number of European countries where Trade Union representations are thought appropriate. Thirdly, there are national and international security problems requiring a sensitive political input which can only be valuable if there is the detailed knowledge to back it up. For example, as Navy Minister I made it my practice to have a meeting with outgoing and incoming British Naval attachés. In this way I gathered much helpful information at first hand about our allies and potential adversaries. I like to think that the attachés found the meetings useful, too, in getting a political feel of their situation.

Similarly, every week I followed the practice that had been going on for many years of a full-scale briefing on the disposition round the world of our ships, their states of readiness and other intelligence information, sometimes of a high security classification. I do not know if either of these routines are continued, but it is clearly three times more difficult for one person to do it for all three Service Boards.

Finally I understand that all the Ministers now sit on all three Service Boards. This means that they can no longer concentrate on single-service high-priority problems, but will tend to become bland arbiters of general policy. In particular, I anticipate that the hitherto sharp discussions on financial matters and new programmes will become blunted, because each Service likes to preserve a few secrets. There is a danger that complete frankness will not be forthcoming at the Army Board on Monday if the Chairman is also to be present at the Navy Board on Thursday.

There is, of course, the argument that Ministers are primarily Ministers of Defence and should not adopt a narrow, parochial outlook. I am sure that this is right and there is a forum, which, if it were properly used, would enable Ministers and others to take the broad view. The Defence Council has as its Chairman the Secretary of State for Defence. Its members include all the Chiefs of Staff, the Defence Ministers, the First Permanent Secretary, the Chief of Defence Procurement and the Chief Scientific Adviser. This may be compared to the main board of a large company which, in many respects, the Ministry of Defence resembles. In that sort of forum the narrow, partisan view is out of place and not indulged in. However, different Defence Secretaries have different impressions about the Council's usefulness and it needs enthusiasm for the concept I have outlined to be successful.

Be that as it may, the post of Navy Minister has gone. I feel that having been the last and following such luminaries as Pepys, Churchill and Hailsham, to name but three, assures me a small place in the history books.

John Nott's recurrent theme in the White Paper, in Parliamentary debates and in the public controversy that has followed has been his claim that increased emphasis on nuclear hunter-killer submarines and Nimrod II maritime patrol aircraft is the real answer to anti-submarine warfare in any NATO conflict in the North Atlantic.

Thus in the White Paper it was stated 'for the future the most cost-effective maritime mix—the best balanced operational contribution for our situation—will be one which continues to enhance our maritime air and submarine effort'.

Since the abolition of separate Service Ministers in the summer of 1981 Mr Nott has continued to justify the cuts. As recently as 13th February 1982 he told the National Young Conservatives Conference at Harrogate that his policy was a 'shift towards a rather smaller surface fleet and support infrastructure, but with more submarines and maritime patrol aircraft'. Even the Falklands conflict does not seem to have shifted him from this line, since in an article in the *Times* on 27th July 1982 he was writing of an increase in 'our nuclear submarine and maritime air capability'.

In fact there are no extra maritime patrol aircraft as a result of the 1981 Defence Review at all. Three additional Nimrod I maritime patrol aircraft, built in the early 1970s, are being modernised to Nimrod IIs. These have the excellent 'searchwater' radar and are a much better electronic bag of tricks than the earlier mark. One aircraft will replace the Nimrod II which was destroyed in a crash at RAF Kinloss in November 1980. The other two are the equivalent to half an aircraft on patrol in the Atlantic 1000 miles away from its base, since it is generally calculated that one on patrol at this range requires four or five aircraft to allow for journeys out and back, maintenance, repairs etc.

I have already commented on the planned number of nuclear hunter-killer submarines being cut by three; one has already been prematurely scrapped. I know that I am not alone when I contrast this so-called increase in air and submarine capability with a reduction of over thirty per cent in the number of major ships in the surface fleet, and their lack of modernisation in the future. However, less than eleven months after my dismissal and only nine months from the Defence White Paper that signalled such drastic cuts in the Royal Navy, the whole of our Defence Policy was to be put to the test in a dramatic way.

8. Battle in the South Atlantic

On 15th December 1981 an 'Early Day Motion' was tabled in the House of Commons which read 'That this House declares its determination that the Falkland Islands and Dependencies shall remain under British Rule in accordance with the wishes of the Islanders and the British interests in the South Atlantic and in the British Antarctic Territories shall be protected and advanced; draws attention to the importance of preserving the international co-operation enshrined in the Antarctic Treaty with particular regard to the conservation and protection of natural resources; and calls upon Her Majesty's Government to demonstrate its commitment to maintaining a tangible presence in the areas by ensuring that the ice patrol ship HMS *Endurance* continues in service after she returns from her current deployment in the spring of 1982 and to achieve these objectives by making the necessary modest savings in public expenditure in other areas which must have a lower order of priority than that of keeping HMS *Endurance* on active service'.

Such motions are rarely debated but provide an important forum for backbench parliamentary opinion. I signed it on the first day it was tabled. By the end of January over 170 MPs from all parties had endorsed it.

The Motion was totally ignored by the Government. Its acceptance would of course have started to erode the basis of the earlier 1981 Defence Review. It should also be noted that *Endurance* was not the 'toothless tiger' she was sometimes made out to be. Apart from carrying twenty or so Royal Marines, who were to give a good account of themselves in South Georgia, she also carried two twenty millimetre cannons plus two Wasp helicopters that could be armed with air-to-surface missiles. In addition she had excellent communications facilities. In fact she was to do superb work in the South Atlantic and to receive a hero's welcome when she returned home to Chatham on 20th August 1982. I was part of the BBC Team which described her moving and enthusiastically received homecoming

117

after nearly eleven months in the South Atlantic.

A few days after this Motion was tabled, on 22nd December 1981, Lieutenant-General Leopoldi Fortunato Galtieri, having carefully made his preparations beforehand, usurped General Videla's place and became Argentina's new President.

The signs which Argentina was at that stage giving of her intention to take the Falkland Islands by force are a matter for speculation. I found when I was Navy Minister that our defence attachés and intelligence services were of a high standard although, like everyone, they could make mistakes. What happened to the information sent by our embassy and intelligence sources is for the independent Committee of Enquiry to investigate. It will presumably also look into the information sent back by Captain Nick Barker, the Commanding Officer of *Endurance*, which during her patrol in South Atlantic waters had visited Argentina.

As I have already mentioned there was a naval debate in parliament on 15th February 1982 when a number of MPs raised the question of the proposed scrapping of HMS *Endurance*. Whether the fact that *Endurance* was on her final patrol, and whether the proposed substantial reductions in the Royal Navy's surface fleet gave a false reading to Buenos Aires I do not know. However, even the keenest supporter of the Government's 1981 Defence policy cannot claim that it helped in any way to deter the Argentinian Junta from the course it was determined to pursue.

Various newspaper reports at home and abroad were hinting that the new head of the Junta was making extremely bellicose noises. After discussions about the Falklands in New York on 26th and 27th February between Argentinian diplomats and British Foreign Office officials headed by Richard Luce, the Minister of State, it was reported that a wide range of options for 'unilateral action' was being considered. Less than three weeks after these talks an Argentine Navy transport auxiliary arrived at Leith, South Georgia's main harbour, and landed a group of Argentinian scrap dealers, illegally as they did not have proper permission or documentation. The *Endurance* was sailed from Stanley in the Falklands to South Georgia but was instructed to lay off the coast as 'diplomatic moves' were taking place. In fact the Argentinian transport ship *Bahia Paraiso*, which carried helicopters and light calibre automatic weapons, arrived at South Georgia and off-loaded supplies.

On Sunday 28th and Monday 29th March newspapers in Britain reported that two Argentinian Corvettes were on their way to South Georgia to protect the *Bahia Paraiso* which was anchored off Leith and being watched by *Endurance*. We now know that during this same weekend other Argentinian ships were on the move, including their aircraft carrier *Veinticinco de Mayo* and a number of escort vessels, all carrying armed marines and soldiers. It is doubtful if many believed the Argentinian cover story that they were off to exercise with the Uruguayan Navy.

On Monday 29th March, we had a debate in the Commons to endorse the Government's decision to maintain a strategic nuclear deterrent and to choose the Trident II Missile system to replace Polaris in due course. This followed the announcement eighteen days earlier by John Nott about Trident II about which I shall say more. It struck me as somewhat bizarre that when there were clearly some 'peculiar goings on' taking place in the South Atlantic, here we were still getting rid of the surface fleet (ex-HMS *Norfolk*, a guided missile destroyer, was on its way to join the Chilean Navy that week) including *Endurance* and at the same time spending eight hours debating a weapon system that was critically important but would not be operational for another thirteen years!

John Nott opened the debate and deployed the case for Trident II. He did not refer to the storm clouds gathering 8000 miles to the South nor did he mention conventional forces except when interrupted by queries from the back benches. However finally I could contain myself no longer. I was certain that the cuts in the conventional Navy taking place at that time, possibly to pay for Trident, could lead to disaster. Accordingly I asked him to give way and I put this question to him: 'Will my Rt Hon. Friend (Mr Nott) answer this riddle which is worrying many people: how can we apparently afford £8000 million to meet a threat in thirteen years' time, which may possibly be true, when we cannot afford £3 million to keep HMS *Endurance* on patrol to meet a threat that is facing us today?'

John Nott replied, '*I do not intend to get involved in a debate about the Falkland Islands now.* These issues are too important to be diverted into a discussion on HMS *Endurance*. In any event as my Hon Friend knows, expenditure on Trident will be extremely small in the next few years.' [18]

Eighty-four hours later, the invasion of the Falklands started with the landing of seventy Argentine Commandos on East Falkland. 'Operacion Rosario', the recapturing of 'the Malvinas', had begun. By the afternoon of the following day, 3rd April, the Falkland Islands and South Georgia were under Argentinian administration and occupation.

The Argentines had overwhelmed the sixty Royal Marines in the Falklands and the twenty in South Georgia who had been landed from *Endurance*. Illegal armed aggression had paid off and 'Operacion Rosario' was successfully concluded.

That Friday 2nd April was a bad, bad day. Confusion seemed to reign in both the Ministry of Defence and the Foreign Office. Such information as was given to Parliament seemed to be both late and inaccurate. Listening to the succession of ever gloomier BBC News reports it appeared that no one in official authority would commit himself to anything until a carrier pigeon had collapsed exhausted on some Whitehall roof. This communication, or rather lack of it, from the South Atlantic was to be a constant source of criticism throughout the campaign and result in an enquiry by the House of Commons Select Committee on defence. This culminated in some harsh words being directed at the public relations set-up of the Ministry.

That evening I was speaking at two Conservative Annual General Meetings in my constituency at the High Halden and St. Michael's branches. Needless to say there was only one subject for the speech and the questions that followed. My supporters shared my sense of shock and outrage. Before I left for my meetings BBC2 Television 'Newsnight' programme telephoned me, very anxious for me to take part in a discussion on the crisis with John Silkin, Labour's Defence Spokesman, and David Owen, then Parliamentary leader of the Social Democratic Party.

On the car journey up to London I had time for a good long think about the situation. It seemed to me that weeping and gnashing of teeth would not help anyone. This was a classic situation for a naval blockade, where ships could first establish a cordon around the islands on and under the sea, later adding an air blockade and an electronic blockade by jamming. The Argentinian occupying forces would need to be supplied with food, fuel, ammunition and all the other myriad stores and spares a modern army needs. Cut off from these supplies they would be softened up either for a diplomatic solution or for an amphibious/helicopter assault. There were it seemed to me three major problems. In order of importance, they were, firstly, lack of air cover over the blockading and amphibious forces while the Argentines could, just, provide air fighter and strike cover from their mainland bases; secondly, the enormous logistical problem of sailing an appropriate fleet 8000 miles with an invading force and their supplies, and keeping them serviced so far from their United Kingdom bases; thirdly, the daunting nature of the coming Antarctic winter with storms, mountainous seas and sub-zero temperatures leading to dangerous wind-chill factors. The last major blockade had taken place twenty years previously and had involved the United States Navy under President John Kennedy's direction but that was in temperate climes, under maritime and airforce air cover and on the United States' back doorstep.

I think it fair to say that the live interview by us three politicians which concluded the programme did provide some hope to the large and influential audience who were watching. As junior member I came in last but put my naval blockade suggestion very strongly. As far as I am aware this was the first time anyone had publicly mentioned such a possibility. I think we all concluded it was an initiative to be pushed while diplomatic talks took place at the same time.

There was certainly no doubt in anyone's mind that the Falklands Campaign was essentially a job for the Royal Navy. On Saturday 3rd April during its first weekend sitting since the 1956 Suez Crisis, Parliament made it clear, with very few dissenting voices, that it would back the twin policies of sending a large task force to the South Atlantic while continuing to negotiate for a peaceful Argentinian withdrawal. A particularly effective and strongly patriotic speech came from the Opposition Leader Michael Foot which drew considerable response from the Government back benches. Within the next few days Britain was to show the world that she was second to none when it came to turning words into action, and on Monday 5th April major units of the fleet sailed from Portsmouth and Devonport to start their long 8000 mile journey, while other ships which were in Gibraltar for the NATO exercises 'Spring Train' were already on their way with a 1000 mile head start. 'Operation Corporate' to retake the Falkland Islands and dependencies was under way.

121

It was clear from the start that the number of Royal Fleet Auxiliary supply ships that would be available would be inadequate to support the massive operation that had been initiated. Matters had not been helped by the reduction of the RFA fleet for reasons of financial economy. Indeed as the fleet sailed, the RFA tanker *Tidepool* was on her way to Chile to join her new owners, the Chilean Navy ... This 27,400 ton displacement tanker, built to fuel warships world-wide and with special structural strengthening for ice operations, was essential, and the Chileans sportingly changed crews with us and let us use the tanker for the duration of the Conflict! She was handed back to Chile at the beginning of August. It was necessary therefore to activate the plans that had been carefully worked out between the Ministry of Defence, the Department of Trade and British merchant shipping companies to charter or requisition a range of ships from passenger liners through tankers and cargo vessels to tugs and trawlers. In all fifty-four merchant ships totalling 673,000 gross registered tons from thirty-three different companies were taken up and they and their crews performed superbly well, carrying over 100,000 tons of freight, 9000 personnel and ninety-five assorted aircraft from Britain to the battle zone.

In the words of the Commander-in-Chief of the Fleet, Admiral Sir John Fieldhouse: 'I cannot say too often or too clearly how important has been the Merchant Navy's contribution to our efforts. Without the ships taken up from trade, the operation could not have been undertaken and I hope this message is clearly understood by the British Nation.' [19]

Since Admiral Fieldhouse was in overall command of the operation, as Commander-in-Chief Fleet, from his headquarters in Northwood, North London, his words have a special significance; Admiral Fieldhouse reported to, and was in constant touch with, the Prime Minister and her 'inner war cabinet'. The Naval task force Commander was Rear Admiral 'Sandy' Woodward who, like Admiral Fieldhouse, is a submarine specialist officer. At the time of the invasion he was in command of the Royal Navy ships at Gibraltar for the exercises in his capacity as Flag Officer First Flotilla (F.O.F.1).

But before this great armada of merchant ships could sail, indeed before the task force sailed itself, a massive amount of work had to be done by the supply and stores organisations, the ship designers, the dockyards and the uniformed services themselves. Ships had to be topped up with war stores and ammunition. Food, drink, clothing for the Antarctic winter, spares for the radars, sonars, weapons and aircraft had to be put on board. Radio sets had to be on top line because during hostilities communications are vital.

An element of luck came into it as well. The carrier *Hermes* was about to begin a refit. A few weeks later and she could not have sailed and *Invincible* would have been insufficient on her own to provide the necessary air cover. The assault ship *Intrepid* had been de-stored and was awaiting paying off in Portsmouth before going into reserve. Thanks to superhuman efforts by all concerned over that April weekend, the fleet, including *Hermes,* sailed on 5th April and *Intrepid* followed two weeks later. One ironic note was the chartering of the four trawlers *Northella, Farnella, Junella* and *Cordella* and their swift conversion into Deep-Sweep Minesweepers. These were to perform the role of the minesweepers (medium) which should have been ordered for the Royal Naval Reserve first in 1980 then in 1981 and had to be delayed indefinitely due to cuts in the Navy's budget.

But it was not only the Royal Navy ships that had to be prepared in a hurry. Many merchant ships had to have helicopter pads added, accommodation altered, communications equipment installed and rigs fitted to allow replenishment at sea. The average time taken was seventy-two hours for 95% of the work in each ship. Gibraltar dockyard took a weekend to convert the luxury cruise liner *Uganda* into a fully-equipped hospital ship ready for use. At any time all this would have been remarkable, but bearing in mind that Chatham and Gibraltar dockyards were due to be closed in less than two years and Portsmouth dramatically run down, while prospective redundancies for these three yards would be many thousands of people, the achievements of the workforce were really outstanding.

Preparations did not end with getting the task force ready for the long voyage and the conflict that followed. A concerted drive was carried out to complete refits as quickly as possible on the warships already in dockyard hands. As the lesson began to be learnt, ships including the refitted Type 42 destroyer *Birmingham* and the newly built Type 42 *Southampton* were leaving refit to go to the South Atlantic and were fitted by the dockyards with extra close-range

123

weapons such as twenty millimetre cannon. In a dramatic reversal of 1981 defence policy the Ministry reprieved from the disposal list six frigates due to be sold or scrapped. The Type 12 frigate *Rhyl* was fitted with extra guns and sailed for the South Atlantic in June. The similar frigates *Berwick* and *Falmouth* were given a hasty refit as were the Type 81 frigates *Tartar, Gurkha* and *Zulu,* and all rejoined the active fleet by the end of July. They would undoubtedly help to plug the yawning gap that had opened in the North Atlantic as so much of the fleet sailed South. Fortunately the conflict was not to be prolonged because there were just no surplus frigates or destroyers waiting in the Royal Navy or indeed in any NATO navy to replace the severe diminution caused by the long journey with the Task Force by so many ships.

This is not the place for a blow-by-blow account of the campaign, but I think one or two general points need to be emphasised before we consider the lessons to be learnt. Whatever the reasons, whatever the lack of actions that directly or indirectly contributed to the invasion, once that first bad day was past, firm political leadership backed by equally resolute public opinion ensured that our forces went into action with the nation united behind them. On 26th April I took part in a Cambridge University Union debate opposing the resolution that 'This House would not be prepared to use force to solve the Falklands Dispute'. My main opponent was Tam Dalyell, Labour MP for West Lothian, who consistently opposed the use of force all the way through. The Motion was defeated by 221 to 81. I believe and indeed the polls showed that, as the campaign went on, support for the Government and the tough line it had taken grew in the country.

The second important point that needs to be made is that Britain won. We mustered a major task force in a matter of hours, sailed it and supported it over 8000 miles away, recapturing South Georgia and the Falkland Islands with the minimum loss of life on both sides and only three civilian casualties. The British have a silly habit of emphasising their defeats and collapsing in a morass of modesty over their victories. Thus we remember Dunkirk, the Dardanelles, Dieppe, Arnhem, Crete, Tobruk and the loss of *Hood,* the *Prince of Wales* and *Repulse* and the escape of the *Scharnhorst, Gneisenau* and *Prinz Eugen.* No doubt in years to come the Falklands battle will chiefly be remembered for the sad loss of *Sheffield* and *Coventry, Ardent, Antelope* and *Atlantic Conveyor* if we run true to form.

By a fortunate accident of geography Ascension Island is roughly halfway between Britain and the Falklands, and the airfield and communications centre developed by the Americans on this British territory enabled ships and aircraft to use the island as a vital 'forward base'. It was nevertheless still 3500 miles away from the battle zone and involved a great deal of flying and steaming.

Admiral Woodward's main problems, both in enforcing a blockade and later in mounting the invasion, centred around his lack of air cover. The Argentinians initially had over one hundred and twenty fast jet aircraft comprising Canberra bombers and Skyhawk, Super Etendard and Mirage III fighter bombers. These were supplemented by forty-five turbo-propeller Pucara ground attack aircraft and a considerable number of modern transport aircraft and helicopters. Apart from the helicopters carried in his ships for anti-submarine, anti-ship and commando rôles, Admiral Woodward started with only twenty-two Sea Harriers in *Hermes* and *Invincible*; these were armed with Sidewinder air-to-air missiles, AIM9L. Later another six Sea Harriers and ten RAF Harrier GR3 Aircraft joined the force, but it was only in the final days of the war when much of the Argentinian Air Force had been destroyed that the numbers of British available aircraft even approached that of the Argentinians.

Admiral Woodward's tactic was clearly to keep his big high value targets as far to the East as possible so that the land based Argentinian aircraft, flying from the West, would have an each way trip of four hundred miles to be over the area of the Islands and more still to attack the carriers or the big liners. At these ranges they were nearing the limits of their endurance, given a few minutes of hard aerial combat.

The defence both of the fleet and the land forces against air attack was based upon different layers at different ranges. Thus the Sea Harriers would be the prime long range interceptors against incoming raiders. This would be backed up by the Sea Dart ship-launched anti-air missiles with ranges up to twenty-five or thirty miles. Sea Dart was carried in the Type 42 destroyers, plus *Bristol* and *Invincible*. Sea Slug, with a range of about eighteen miles, was an earlier generation ship-launched anti-air missile carried in the 'County' Class destroyers. Then the much shorter range Sea Cat system effective up to about three miles with various operator controlled or automatic radar guidance on to the target. These were carried in *Hermes*, the Type 21 frigates, the Type 12 frigates and the 'Batch 2 Leander Class frigates'. Then at a slightly shorter range still the very modern and effective Sea Wolf missile system designed to destroy incoming missiles and shells was carried in the Type 22 frigates and the Batch 3 Leander frigate *Andromeda*.

To supplement all this were a number of twenty millimetre cannon fitted to most ships, either as standard equipment or specially for the conflict, plus assorted machine guns to give moral support as much as anything else, although certainly a number of aircraft were brought down by these light weapons. In addition the Type 42 destroyers and Type 12 and 21 frigates had 4.5 inch guns which had three tasks: land bombardment or 'naval gunfire support'; action against surface ships, and medium to short range defence against air attack.

It is doubtful if the true Argentinian air losses will ever be revealed. Apart from those seen to be destroyed in the air and on the ground there were almost certainly a number damaged that did not get back to their bases. At the start of the conflict the Argentinian Air Force strength including helicopters, naval aircraft and military transport totalled approximately 320. Not all these could be thrown into the battle because of guerrilla and insurgency threats in other parts of the country. However by 6th August 1982 the British Ministry of Defence estimated that 109 Argentinian aircraft had been destroyed including thirty-one out of seventy-four Skyhawks and twenty-six out of fifty-three Mirages. To lose over one third of their combined airforce and naval air arm and approaching a half of their main fighters and fighter bombers, to say nothing of a large number of brave, skilled and experienced jet pilots, must be counted a military disaster, and one that will take years to make good. According to the Ministry of Defence's analysis, Harriers accounted for twenty-seven aircraft destroyed, the land based Rapier missile system for thirteen, Sea Dart for eight, Sea Cat for six and Sea Wolf for five. However, individual numbers between missile systems and guns should be treated with some caution. In addition forty-two aircraft were found destroyed on the ground.

The Sea Harrier proved itself as a truly remarkable multi-rôle combat aircraft. Altogether 1500 sorties were flown by the twenty-eight Sea Harriers and 150 sorties by the ten RAF Harrier GR3s. No aircraft were downed in aerial combat, the five losses sustained by Sea Harriers and Harrier GR3s were due to ground fire. Armed with the later versions of the Sidewinder missile and operating its Ferranti 'Blue Fox' attack radar the Sea Harrier is a formidable and all-weather fighter. Highly manoeuvrable, using its vectored thrust it can make sudden changes of course and speed to confuse an attacker or incoming missile. It converts easily to the strike rôle and can carry a good payload of bombs and rockets to strafe enemy targets; so great was the reliability of the aircraft, its weapons and radar that Sea Harriers were able to carry out over 99 per cent of the missions assigned to them in the South Atlantic, while its low loss rate by enemy action, coupled with a very high rate of serviceability and reliability, enabled it to achieve continuous high intensity flying throughout the conflict. This helped Admiral Woodward to make up to some extent the great disparity in numbers between his fighter/strike aircraft and the Argentinians' – an adverse ratio of about three to one.

Apart from the air battle Admiral Woodward could not neglect either the surface or the sub-surface naval threat. The Argentinian fleet was a mixed bag of old and new British and American built ships. The aircraft carrier *Veinticinco de Mayo* (which started life as HMS *Venerable* and was a sister ship to HMS *Ocean* which I served in as a midshipman, later became the Netherlands *Karel Doorman* and was extensively refitted when she was bought from the Dutch) carried Skyhawk jet strike planes and super Etendard jet aircraft armed with air-launched Exocet missiles, and posed a considerable threat to the task force. The pre-war USS *Phoenix*, a 14,000 ton cruiser with fifteen six-inch guns and many smaller guns and missiles, had become the *General Belgrano* and carried the largest guns on any ship in either navy. Two of the Argentinian destroyers were British designed, Types 42, one built at Vickers, Barrow, the other in the Argentine. These two, the *Hercules* and the *Santisima Trinidad*, were consequently armed with the Sea Dart missile system.

This fleet together with other older or smaller surface escort ships, some armed with Exocet surface-to-surface missiles, which were not to be discounted, posed a problem in enforcing the blockade or 'total exclusion zone' as it was called. The *General Belgrano* on 2nd May escorted by two destroyers was outside this zone, but heading for it and closing on advanced isolated units of the task force. As the USS *Phoenix* she had survived the Japanese attack on

Pearl Harbor in 1941. Just over forty years later her life came to an end when she was torpedoed by the nuclear powered hunter-killer submarine HMS *Conqueror* with old fashioned straightforward cheap Mark 8 torpedoes. She remained afloat for less than an hour and several hundred men were lost. The effect of this plus some pretty strong psychological warfare meant that the main units of the Argentinian surface fleet remained bottled up in their ports while an undisclosed number of British submarines, probably but not necessarily all nuclear powered, maintained an effective blockade outside them.

There was still however the submarine threat to be dealt with. Argentina possessed four submarines. Two of these were old United States 'Guppy' designs of 2540 tons with an eighteen knot underwater speed, diesel electric driven with considerable range. Their armament was the old pre-war designed U.S. Mark 14 Mod 5 torpedo which is not too dissimilar to the Royal Navy's Mark 8 that sunk the *Belgrano*; each submarine had ten torpedo tubes. One of these boats, the *Santa Fe*, was beached and severely damaged by RN helicopters which fired at her when she was sighted approaching South Georgia, just before the island was recaptured by Britain. The whereabouts of the other one, the *Santiago del Estero*, remained a mystery until it was established that she had been unserviceable for a long time and was being cannibalised for spare parts for the *Santa Fe*.

The other two boats, the *San Luis* and the *Salta*, were modern, German built, with a dived tonnage of 1285, a fast underwater speed from their batteries of up to twenty-two knots and each armed with sixteen West German modern SST-4 wire-guided acoustic homing torpedoes similar to the Royal Navy's Tigerfish Mark 24 type. The drawback with these boats is that they are essentially coastal submarines designed more for short patrols in the Baltic or Northern Europe rather than long patrols in the South Atlantic. However with a determined if suicidal commander, and with the difficult water conditions for good sonar operation in the South Atlantic either of these boats could have posed the greatest danger to the British carriers or the *Q.E.2* or *Canberra*.

That they did not achieve any success at all must be due in no small part to the excellent anti-submarine screening work done by the frigates of the task force together with the Sea King anti-submarine warfare helicopters from the carriers. I have no doubt that nuclear-powered and conventional submarines were used in an important anti-submarine rôle as well by the Task Force Commander. The political and military consequences if these anti-submarine elements had lifted their guard and allowed a successful attack on a prime target would have been incalculable.

When the amphibious landing in Falkland Sound off Port San Carlos started on 21st May there were prime targets a-plenty for the Argentinian Airforce. The luxury liner *Canberra*, the amphibious warfare ships *Fearless* and *Intrepid* plus a host of other transports, frigates and destroyers were not only defending themselves against air attack but firing hundreds of 4.5 inch shells ashore to give accurate gunfire support for the invading forces.

In the seventy-two hours between 21st and 24th May the Royal Navy was to lose two Type 21 frigates *Ardent* and *Antelope*. *Ardent* was riddled with high explosive rockets fired by Argentinian Mirages and had to be abandoned with twenty-two of her crew killed. I am saddened by the loss of any ship and the deaths of any servicemen but I felt a particular wrench at the loss of *Ardent*. She was the last RN ship I visited while still Navy Minister. I went aboard her to welcome her back from a Gulf of Oman patrol on St. George's day, 23rd April 1981, and was impressed both by the ship and her crew.

On 23rd May *Antelope* was hit by a bomb from a Sky Hawk which was itself shot down moments later. The bomb did not explode but lodged in the engine room from which the Rolls Royce Olympus and Tyne gas turbines drive the ship. The Royal Engineer who tried to defuse the bomb was killed when it went off and despite all efforts by the crew, the ship had to be abandoned; the explosion and fire beat them. But the loss of these two ships must be seen against the incredible feat of landing over 5000 troops together with all their equipment and not losing a single soldier. The *Antelope* and *Ardent* had to stay put, for operational reasons, off San Carlos in the Falkland Sound. Thus they could not make use of their main assets, speed and manoeuvrability, as the waters of the Sound are very restrictive and allow little 'sea room'. Their task was to defend the landing force and provide the essential softening up gunfire support. Their sacrifice was not in vain.

I shall explore later some of the technical problems and lessons to be learnt from the conflict and not least from the losses of *Sheffield* and *Atlantic Conveyor*, both destroyed by Exocet missiles. But with

129

the battle won and the Falkland Islands and their people once more under British administration there are a number of specific points relevant to the South Atlantic that need to be made.

There was, in my view rightly, widespread criticism of the way that news was handled by the Ministry and the long delay in getting visual information to British television screens. It is ironic that in an era of supersonic missiles and aircraft in conflict, with satellite communication and with electronic news-gathering equipment, there was a total lack of urgency or indeed understanding about the best use of television in a campaign of this kind.

At the risk of being accused of labouring a point I believe this is another casualty that springs from the decision to abolish single-service Ministers. The Secretary of State, in a major conflict involving Britain's armed forces, is clearly too busy to have a detailed day-to-day knowledge of what is happening on the inform-ation front. His appearances and involvement should be reserved only for the most important and fundamental matters of policy or announcements to be made. His junior Navy, Army or Air Force Minister, in my view, should be responsible for the overall direction of information to the public, to relatives of the servicemen, to our Allies, and to 'world opinion' which may well be adopting an anti-British view.

In the Falklands case this person would clearly have been the Navy Minister, backed up by the appropriate Chiefs of Staff; in other conflicts it could well be other Ministers.

As a politician with detailed and expert knowledge of the major Service involved I believe that the whole public presentation could have been handled a sight more efficiently and sensitively. I much regret that single-service Ministers no longer exist, and that Chiefs of Staff can be 'seen but not heard' since, as was widely reported, they are now no longer allowed to address the Back Bench House of Commons defence committees when invited to do so.

The second important point has been much debated and concerns the prospective ability of Britain to mount a comparable task force had the invasion of the Falklands taken place in, say, 1984 and not 1982. Ministers have stated that we would have been just as prepared but I believe that this claim is open to strong challenge. Based on Mr Nott's original 1981 policy, by 1984 only the carriers *Hermes* and *Illustrious* would have been in service, *Invincible* having been sold to Australia. I do not believe fortune would have smiled on us so sweetly a second time and ensured that two out of two carriers would have been immediately available for operations. I cannot stress too strongly that to give a reasonable guarantee of two carriers being available at short notice, three are needed in the fleet. That is why the 'Invincible' class consists of three ships, *Invincible*, *Illustrious* and the yet to be completed *Ark Royal*.

Both the amphibious warfare ships *Fearless* and *Intrepid* which played such a vital rôle in the Falklands would not have been operational in two years' time. Although they had been reprieved from being scrapped just before the crisis almost certainly one would have been in reserve in 1984 and it would have taken considerable time to have brought it back into service. A number of escorts like the Leander frigates, *Bristol* and the 'County' class destroyers would have left the fleet. HMS *Endurance* would have been disposed of, so would several more urgently needed Royal Fleet Auxiliary Support Ships. Even if the Navy could have overcome all these deficiencies, especially those concerned with the all-important carrier provisions, there still is the question of back-up support.

The 1981 White Paper said 'We shall have to close a substantial number of naval stores and fuel depots'. Three years later they would have gone. By 1984 Chatham and Gibraltar dockyards and naval bases would have been closed and Portsmouth dockyard would have been a shadow of its former self. Where all the ship conversion, storing, fuelling, ammunition and structural alterations could have been done is never mentioned. Equally obscure is who would do them since it was necessary in 1982 in order to prepare the Falklands fleet to suspend all dockyard redundancy notices at Chatham, Portsmouth and Gibraltar even before the major redundancies had started. Finally it should not be forgotten that not only would the 1981 Nott plans call for civilian supporting staff to be cut by well over 10,000 by 1984, but the Navy would be about 7000 officers and ratings less than in 1982 as well, as part of a planned reduction of 10,000 by 1986.

The *Sunday Times* on 5th September 1982 reported comments by the First Sea Lord Admiral Sir Henry Leach 'labelling as a pack of lies Ministerial claims that Britain could repeat a Falklands type exercise in 1985 or 1990'. He as the professional serving officer leading the Navy should know.

131

Having successfully concluded 'Operation Corporate' and won the war it is now important for us to keep the peace. There are many imponderables for us to consider. The stability of the Junta is, to say the least, precarious, with probably the one person who emerged with honour from the war, the Air Force Commander Brigadier Lami Dozo, having left it on 17th August 1982 and General Galtieri having been deposed several weeks earlier. Can democracy or at any rate a more liberal and far-sighted administration come to Argentina? Is there any prospect for some kind of concordat between the littoral states of the South Atlantic plus perhaps Britain and the United States? Alternatively, and less likely, has the United Nations or the Organisation of American States a rôle to play in guaranteeing the freedom and integrity of the Falkland Islands and their dependencies? Can Britain have a partnership with Argentina for the commercial development of the fish in, and the minerals under, the seas around the Falklands, or will the scars from the conflict run too deep?

Whatever the answer to these conundrums, indeed if there is any answer, Britain will for the indefinite future have to provide sufficient land, air and sea forces to safeguard the Falklands from surprise attack. Sufficient that is to ensure that any invasion or blockade attempt could meet with effective and sustained opposition until more powerful back-up forces were brought into play. It is of course a matter for military judgment as to the minimum level of these forces. I would envisage good air defences with Rapier missiles on the islands; at least a squadron of Phantom fighter aircraft armed with air-to-air missiles would be necessary, plus probably a squadron of Harriers which would be vital if the runway at Stanley airport were destroyed. High quality surface and air radar giving timely warning of approaching vessels and aircraft would be needed together with a permanent garrison of at least a battalion of troops plus those necessary for backing up the air defences and civil engineering work.

On the naval side there must be at least one or more nuclear or conventional submarines always in the area although exact numbers are not and should not be revealed. Two or three appropriately equipped ships should be there to back them up. Batch 3 type Leander frigates which are armed with Exocet surface-to-surface and Sea Wolf surface-to-air missiles would be ideal. These would operate with a Type 42 destroyer with 4.5 inch gun and long range Sea Darts, both types having a reasonable anti-submarine capability and using Lynx helicopters. In addition a Royal Fleet Auxiliary and RFA Freighter will be needed to keep the ships and aircraft and garrison supplied with fuel, ammunition and stores. Apart from acting as a useful deterrent against attack these ships and submarines could carry out exercises together. The training can be as realistic, cold, uncomfortable and valuable in the South Atlantic as that carried out in the North Atlantic.

Finally the success of the immense Falkland Islands undertaking underlines the prime importance of balanced flexible maritime forces. The submarines, the carriers, the fixed wing aircraft and helicopters, the surface escort ships, the amphibious warfare ships, the minesweepers, the tankers, the supply ships, the despatch vessels, the repair vessels and tugs, all had a vital rôle to play and all were interdependent one with another.

The whole point is that if one or more elements of this balance are removed the capability of the whole is jeopardised. Perhaps the Falklands crisis came just in time to remind us of this essential truth of maritime warfare, a truth that Gorshkov the Russian Admiral understands well, as I have already shown, and a truth which we ignore at our peril.

9. The Missile War— Are Surface Ships Obsolete?

The maritime Missile war probably started on 21st October 1967. On that day, ironically enough Trafalgar Day, the Russian built 'Komar' Class missile boats of the Egyptian Navy fired their 'Styx' missiles from inside Alexandria Harbour at the Israeli Naval Ship *Eilath*, which was patrolling out at sea, and sank her. This action, a relatively simple one in itself, was to make many navies think furiously about their surface armament. Britain did not have an adequate surface-to-surface missile, although the Sea Slug II being fitted to the later 'County' Class destroyers and the new Sea Dart then being developed would have some anti-ship performance. Really, though, they were anti-air missiles.

In 1970 the new Conservative Government decided to purchase from France the Exocet MM38 ship-launched anti-ship missile, with a 40 kilometre range. These missiles were to be fitted in some of the 'County' Class destroyers, the Type 21 and 22 Class frigates and some of the 'Leander' Class frigates on modernisation. The Falklands battle however was to involve the full range of surface-to-surface, surface-to-air, air-to-air and air-to-surface missiles as well as electronic wizardry, 'chaff' decoys and good old-fashioned guns.

One of the vital factors that Admiral Woodward had to take in to account when he began the Falklands operation was the lack of airborne early warning radar. This takes us back to Denis Healey's Defence Review of 1966, as I have shown, and his decision not to proceed with the new generation of aircraft carriers. While the Royal Navy had conventional carriers operating propeller-driven aeroplanes the latter could carry a powerful radar set which could extend the 'eyes and ears' of the Fleet by a hundred miles or so. First, in the 1950s, these were the piston-engined Douglas Skyraider and later, in the 1960s and '70s, the twin turbo-propeller Fairey Gannet which operated at a height of thousands of feet. These aeroplanes would carry a powerful radar set and fly a patrol on a predetermined pattern, transmitting radar-gathered information about ships or aircraft that could be approaching a task force. A radar set works at a very high frequency and its range is really line-of-sight. Thus, within limits, the higher above ground the aerial, the greater the range of the set. Since the average ship's radar aerial is perhaps eighty feet above the sea, obviously an aerial at eight thousand feet, in an aeroplane, will have a much greater range. Equally important, since the radar 'looks down' from the aircraft, it can spot incoming aircraft or missiles that might be flying very low to come in under the radar beams of the surface ships.

The current United States carriers each have a four plane detachment of Grumman twin turboprop 'Hawkeye' aircraft. These carry a huge radar aerial like a meat plate above the fuselage and can provide effective all-round radar coverage out to a range of 240 nautical miles. Unfortunately there is no way that this aeroplane, nor indeed the Fairey Gannet, could be operated from *Invincible* and *Hermes*, with their ski-jumps and flight decks specially prepared for the v/STOL Sea Harriers. So Admiral Woodward had to do without airborne early warning radar. The loss of HMS *Sheffield* on 4th May was, I believe, largely due to this lack. We know that she was hit by a French Exocet AM39 missile which was launched by an Argentinian Naval Super Etendard aircraft from a range of about twenty-five miles. The pilot controls it from his radar screen in the cockpit and, in the later stages of its flight, the missile's own radar guides it on to the target. Once it has been launched it drops down until it is just a few feet above the surface of the sea, which it 'skims' at speeds of up to Mach 0.9, like a flying fish. In fact the name Exocet is a corruption of 'Exocoetidae' which is the Family name of flying fish.

We know that it was the enormous kinetic energy of some 1200 lb of missile travelling at about 670 m.p.h., plus an explosion caused by the unburnt propellant fuel in the missile and not the high explosive warhead, that did the mortal damage to *Sheffield*. The Commanding Officer estimated he had only about twenty seconds' warning of the approach of the missile. This did not leave him time to take the appropriate electronic counter measures to jam the Exocet's radar or to fire 'chaff' from the ship's launchers. 'Chaff' is a cloud of small, carefully cut strips of aluminium, very like the tinsel on a Christmas tree. These deceive the missile's radar into thinking that the cloud of shimmering chaff is the target and the missile is seduced away accordingly. With good warning these anti-missile passive defence systems can work very effectively, as a number of ships in the Falklands proved since at least four air-launched Exocet missiles are believed to have been discouraged away from their targets during the campaign.

The loss of *Sheffield* was not only a bad blow to the Task Force but it shook the country and Parliament, and many people realised for the first time that modern conventional warfare was every bit as bloody as the horrors of nuclear war. Although a number of naval ships and lives had been lost due to accidents since 1945, and many had been damaged in various operational activities, including the Korean War and the 'confrontation' with Indonesia in the 1960s, *Sheffield* was the first to be lost by direct hostile enemy action since the Second World War—and it hurt.

Unfortunately for the Task Force the Nimrod 3 Airborne Early Warning Aircraft were not due to enter service until 1983 and there would not be ten fully operational until 1985. Their nearest air base at Ascension Island is about 3400 miles away so there would be a round trip of over sixteen hours just to get there and back, plus extra time for flight refuelling, and the time on task would be limited. To maintain one aircraft constantly on patrol would tie up about eight aircraft, or virtually the entire fleet of Nimrod 3s when they enter service in 1985, to say nothing of a considerable number of VC10 tanker aircraft as well!

Quite clearly, not only in the Falklands conflict but in any possible maritime hostilities away from our shores it is a dangerous presumption to rely upon any kind of airborne early warning, apart from what the fleet has itself. Matters were not helped in *Sheffield*'s case by her own air warning radar set being the 965 type which was original equipment when she was completed in 1974. This set has been replaced by the 1022 radar in more recent ships because the former is inadequate to deal with the modern threat. Better developments are still coming along. *Sheffield*, first of its Class, was due to have a mid-life refit and modernisation in the mid 1980s when much equipment would have been modernised and updated. However this mid-life modernisation programme for the Royal Navy was scrapped as part of the 1981 Navy cuts and the need to close the dockyards to save money.

I am sure that I was not alone in thinking hard about the airborne radar problem as an aftermath of the loss of *Sheffield*. When as Navy Minister I had visited Westland Helicopters at Yeovil in 1980 I had seen, while walking round the factory, some Sea King helicopters stuffed with electronic equipment for a foreign customer. Lord Aldington, the Westlands Chairman, was a good friend, a constituent and President of the Ashford Conservative Association. I rang him and asked if it were possible to put a suitable radar set in a Sea King Helicopter and use the ensemble as a rotary wing airborne early warning system. He thought it was, but sensibly put me in touch with Dr Jones, Westland's Technical Director, to whom I spoke on 17th May. He was keen on the idea, saw no major problems and thought a conversion could be done in a few months. I passed the concept on with Westlands' blessing to the Ministry of Defence on the same day.

On 6th August 1982, Desmond Wettern, the knowledgeable naval correspondent of the *Daily Telegraph* wrote:

> The problem of giving defending fighters warning of approaching aircraft has been overcome in only eleven weeks with the conversion of two Sea King anti-submarine helicopters into early warning aircraft. Both are now on their way South to the Falklands, on board the new carrier *Illustrious*, 19,500 tons, which is to relieve her sister ship *Invincible* later this month.
>
> The speed with which the conversion was completed by Westland Helicopters who make the Sea King and Thorn-EMI who produce the helicopters' 'Searchwater' radar, which is also fitted in the latest RAF Nimrod maritime patrol aircraft, has won them high praise from the Defence Ministry. The conversion of the Sea Kings for their new rôle stems at least partly from a proposal put forward by the former Navy Minister, Mr Keith Speed, after the loss of the destroyer *Sheffield* on May 4th.

I have already described how air defence should be in depth, with fighters at farthest range, then long-, medium- and short-range guns and missiles. The trouble was that we had insufficient Sea Harriers to maintain large numbers of aircraft in the air on 'combat air patrol'. If there had been airborne early warning radar aircraft available these could have given long-range advance warning of incoming raiders and allowed sufficient time for more Sea Harriers to take off and intercept the attackers long before they reached the ships. Good aircraft direction from the ships was vital to direct your aircraft into the most favourable attacking position, but this again relies on good radar, so that accurate information on ranges and heights can be used by the controllers. This lesson of good radar coupled with expert aircraft direction was one we and the Germans learned forty-two years earlier in the Battle of Britain. Once the Sea Harriers got close to their target they could use their own 'Blue Fox' radar to intercept and attack with missiles or cannon shells.

The Sea Dart missile system, like Exocet, was possessed by both sides, as the Argentinians had it fitted in their two Type 42 destroyers. This meant that they knew its characteristics and would plan their attacks to avoid it if at all possible. However, it also meant that the Argentine surveillance planes, essential properly to direct the Super Etendards with their airborne Exocets, were kept well away and prevented from flying high at effective ranges. Thus the single high-value targets like the *Canberra* troopship or the two carriers were not damaged and there is some evidence that the pilots of the Etendards chose what appeared to be the largest target on their radar screens, fired their missiles and got the hell out. This perhaps explains the loss, on 25th May, of the container ship *Atlantic Conveyor* which had to be abandoned after being hit by an Exocet. The reconnaissance aircraft were kept at bay and attacking aircraft forced by the long range Sea Dart into flight profiles they might otherwise have avoided or into flight levels where the Harriers or other weapon systems could wrest the advantage. In other words Sea Dart forced them often to fly where we wanted them, rather than where they wished to fly themselves. It is just a very great pity that plans to up-date what is already a good weapon system had to be cancelled in 1981 because of the cuts in the Navy's finances. But more modern surveillance radar like the Type 1022, which has a better range and definition of the target, and several new models being developed will help to improve the system as a whole.

At this point it is worth dealing with widespread misunderstandings that have been fostered and encouraged by some whose motives are obscure. Allegations have been made that it is only due to the incompetence of the Argentinian Air Force and their ordnance branch that half the fleet was not sunk, since many ships were hit by bombs which did not explode. These allegations are not only false but they do not do justice to the bravery and skill either of the Argentinian Airforce or of the Royal Navy. No doubt some bombs and fuses were faulty; it would be remarkable if this were not so. But the essential point that has been missed is that enemy aircraft were forced by our long and short range missile and gun defence systems to fly, in many cases, at suicidally low levels in order to deliver the bombs at all without being shot down beforehand. This meant that bombs were being dropped only – and literally – a few feet above their targets, as everyone saw on the remarkable television coverage of, for example, the attack on ships in the Falkland Sound off San Carlos. The interval between the bomb's release and its hitting the thin steel of the ship is so short, maybe fractions of a second, that the fuse which explodes it does not have time to 'arm'. This is an essential built-in safety measure, so that if the bomb is released accidentally while the aircraft is on the ground, or on the carrier, it does not explode. Similarly, when released in combat it ensures that it does not explode prematurely and send to Kingdom Come the aeroplane that has just released it. It was all summed up very neatly in a letter to me after the battle from Captain David Pentreath who had been commanding HMS *Plymouth* which was hit by a number of bombs that did not explode: 'Thank God so many of their bombs failed to fuse—because they adopted very low attack profiles, attempting to avoid our missile envelopes.' In *Plymouth*'s case 'they' were not very successful because she shot down two Mirage fighters, one with a Sea Cat missile and one with a gun!

The Sea Wolf close-range missile became a household word in a matter of weeks. I was often asked why the system was not being fitted to every ship in the Royal Navy from tugs upwards. The questioner looked surprised when told it cost money, millions of pounds for each system, and the existing 'heavyweight' Sea Wolf weighs about forty-two tons for the two six-barrelled launchers and tracker radars normally installed in a ship, plus another thirteen tons or so for all the computers, control gear and associated equipment. Sea Wolfs are fitted as standard equipment into Type 22 frigates, with two complete six-barrel launcher systems placed one forward of the bridge and one aft of the main mast above the helicopter hangar. The 'Batch 3 Leander' class frigates, on major modernisation, are similarly fitted. There were, during the battle, two or three

Type 22s and a Leander who took with Sea Wolf a toll not only of enemy aircraft at short range, but of incoming missiles as well. The story of the Sea Wolf development is long and complex and it is frankly a wonder that the weapon survived the plethora of committees, Whitehall in-fighting, international non-cooperation, technical problems and lack of single-ministry direction. But survive all these drawbacks it did. The project started with a naval concept study in 1962 and French and Dutch interest which by the time of the British project definition, in 1965, had evaporated. The Admiralty Surface Weapons Establishment (ASWE) were reported as wanting to lead the project, so were the British Aircraft Corporation (British Aeroplane Division). The idea of vertical launching, which had considerable operational advantages (because the launch tubes could be fitted in the deck and the missiles launched in any direction and reloaded under cover), was rejected for reasons of technical risk and because the missile to be used would probably be more expensive. The various problems were eventually solved, although the equipment developed was very heavy. The missile first went to sea operationally in HMS *Broadsword* in 1978, with the GWS25 Marconi radar system, the missiles themselves made by British Aerospace Dynamics and the launchers by Vickers.

However, much work had been going into a lightweight Sea Wolf and also into an enhanced radar capability to deal more effectively with sea-skimming missiles like Exocet or the Russian SSN-2-C. This led to the development of a system weighing not forty-two but sixteen tons. It was much smaller, too, and there was the possibility that it could be put in an easy-to-maintain container, on to merchant ships for self defence as well as on to warships. British Aerospace, in co-operation with Signaal, the Dutch Radar Company, using their VM40 radar, completed a series of successful firing and tracking trials of the new weapon in 1980 and 1981 and both the Dutch and British firms, as well as the Ministry, had put considerable sums of money into the development. Plans were also made whereby parts of the Dutch radar could be made in the United Kingdom, thus retaining jobs within the Marconi group.

However, Marconi were putting together their own package and were already concerned about naval cuts and the loss of research and design staff should the VM40 Dutch radar package be ordered. Much lobbying of Members of Parliament, the Ministry and press took place by all concerned. After a fair bit of delay it was announced, in 1982, that an all-British lightweight Sea Wolf would be developed using the Marconi SW805 radar.

It is hoped by the Ministry that this new lightweight system will be operational by 1984, although if past experience is anything to go by that seems somewhat optimistic. British Aerospace did not exactly welcome this decision with open arms. As far as they were concerned they had a good system that worked. Using a proven Dutch radar already being sold to various navies would help export prospects, not least with the Dutch. So they are continuing to develop and offer lightweight Sea Wolf VM40 and believe they have excellent prospects for it. It is certainly a couple of years ahead of the all-British version but the RN and British Merchant Fleets will not be using VM40! After all the previous problems, British Aerospace are going ahead with developing a vertical launcher once more, which will be the next significant development.

In the meantime the Sea Wolf missile is the only effective and proven anti-aircraft and anti-missile system with a range approaching four miles, a speed of Mach two and the capacity to hit a 4.5 inch shell or missile in flight. In its lightweight new radar version it will deal even more effectively with the sea-skimming missile threat and it can be put in a container pack aboard tankers or other unsophisticated ships. I certainly expect it to be standard equipment for the new Type 23 frigate due to enter service in the Royal Navy by 1989. I hope too that it can be fitted in 'sponsons' (built-on bays out from the ship's side carrying the weapon) to the three 'Invincible' Class carriers, to back up the Sea Dart air defence system that they already have.

The first missile casualty of the war was the Argentine submarine *Santa Fé* which was making for South Georgia on 25th April and was crippled by an AS12 air-to-surface missile fired by one of HMS *Endurance*'s Wasp helicopters. One new missile which had not even been declared operational when the Task Force sailed scored the second missile success of the Falklands War. On the 2nd May, the same day the *General Belgrano* was torpedoed, a Sea King helicopter on anti-submarine patrol in foul weather conditions was fired on by the Argentinian armed tugs *Comodoro Somellera* and *Alferez Sobral*. Lynx helicopters were called up from the escort frigates and destroyers. In a dark night, with a high sea running, they located the

Argentinian ships with their 'Sea Spray' radar and carried out text book attacks with the new sea-skimming Sea Skua anti-ship missiles. This was the first ever operational firing and conditions could not have been worse. The rough sea, with high waves, meant a high profile flight for the missiles, so that they cleared the waves and did not disappear into their crests. Notwithstanding this, one missile sank the *Comodoro Somellera* and the other badly damaged the *Alferez Sobral*. Sea Skua is designed as a weapon to be fitted to helicopters to destroy or damage small surface vessels, including fast attack craft, in reasonable seas. I have no doubt it will add significantly to the striking power of the Lynx helicopter, provided that they are left by the Defence Review with enough decks to operate from.

In view of the success of the Exocet missile in sinking *Sheffield* and *Atlantic Conveyor* when launched from the air, and in damaging *Glamorgan* when launched from the shore, many people have wondered why there is not a British equivalent. I have already listed the surface Royal Naval ships that are fitted with Exocet and a number of British firms are involved, on a sub-contract basis, in its manufacture. However, British Aerospace are developing a new air-launched missile which will be superior to Exocet in virtually all regards. This is called Sea Eagle and is an anti-ship missile which will be carried by RAF Buccaneers and Tornado strike aircraft and Royal Naval Sea Harriers. There were reports of a considerable shadow over its future for a time in 1981 while defence cuts were being planned. Certainly at one stage the Navy seemed to be much keener on its development and production than anyone else. However, it has now been given the green light and is being jointly funded by the RAF and the RN, with the RAF paying the lion's share. A shipborne version called P5T is a possibility and would be an obvious replacement in due course for the Exocet missiles currently fitted.

All this heady talk of missiles should not disguise the very important rôle that guns had to play in the Falklands and have to play in naval strategy everywhere. HMS *Alacrity*, a Type 21 frigate, demonstrated on the night of the 11th May the use of guns in their traditional rôle against other surface ships when she was on patrol in the Falkland Sound between East and West Falkland. Her radar detected a surface target which tried to escape. Several radar-controlled shots from her Mark 8 4.5 inch gun hit the contact, which exploded in an enormous ball of flame. Later it was learnt that the vessel that had been so summarily destroyed was the Argentine Auxiliary supply ship *Islas do Los Estados* which was trying to sneak supplies through to Argentinian garrisons under cover of darkness. These 4.5 inch guns also showed their worth in traditional bombardment of the land in naval gunfire support of the troops. During the campaign over 8000 4.5 inch shells were fired at Argentinian land targets and all the indications are that this gunfire was extremely accurate and also that it contributed significantly to the collapse of morale among the Argentinian military.

Guns were also, of course, being used for anti-air attack, and are immensely valuable particularly as close-in weapons to defend the ship at very short range. Both the 4.5 inch and the 40 and 20 millimetre quick-firing guns all gave a good account of themselves against attacking aircraft and, together with the missiles, forced them to fly at heights that caused problems with bomb fuses and with aircraft control. Several aeroplanes were seen to dive into the sea, apparently without being hit, after taking violent avoiding action and at least one incoming Exocet missile, fired from a Super Etendard, was destroyed after being hit by a 4.5 inch shell fired by HMS *Avenger* in early June 1982.

I referred earlier, in Chapter Eight, to the concept of layered air defence to protect a task force and it is clear that guns have an important rôle to play in it. Indeed many ships fitted additional machine guns and twenty millimetre cannon to supplement their standard armament, and warships sailing to reinforce the fleet had additional 20 millimetre guns fitted at great speed by the dockyards. The mounting of additional guns, however, is something that has to be considered most carefully. In the heat of battle, an enthusiastic gunner might swing his weapon round and shoot away his own ship's mast or funnel if they are sited wrongly! Ammunition storage, too, both for immediate and long term use, has to be provided and all this extra metal can affect the ship's magnetic 'signature' and thus make her more susceptible to certain kinds of mines.

The lack of any short range air defence system on the 'Invincible' Class carriers bothered me as a Minister and bothered me through the Falklands battle. It was my intention, as I hinted to Parliament in 1980, that *Invincible*, on her first major refit, should have light-weight Sea Wolf fitted in sponsons at bow and stern. In due course *Illustrious* and *Ark Royal* would follow suit and I also hoped that we would fit extra guns as a close-in weapon system. Before the Falklands crisis blew up there was little money available for this kind of improvement. We were all wise after the event, however, and HMS *Illustrious*, at the start of her first commission in July 1982, was fitted with two sets of Phalanx close-in shipboard weapon systems, one forward and one aft. These are highly effective, firing 3000 rounds per minute from a radar-directed multi-gun system, and are for defence against low-flying aircraft and missiles that are heading close in to the ship. Made by the Pomona Divison of the General Dynamics Corporation of America they are to be installed in some 240 ships by the United States Navy.

I hope we can see the Phalanx fitted in *Invincible* soon and in *Ark Royal* before she is completed, so that all three carriers, together with the assault ships *Fearless* and *Intrepid* are equipped with this potent defence system. This would mean that in due course the carriers would have long-range Sea Dart and short-range Sea Wolf surface-to-air missiles, plus Phalanx guns as close-in weapons, and this would make them much less vulnerable to air attack.

The 'short hull' Type 42 destroyers certainly do not have room for light-weight Sea Wolf and there must be a question mark over whether they have space for the Phalanx system with its radar, guns and ammunition storage, without giving up something else. What is clear beyond doubt is that these ships need a back-up short-range air-defence system and a possible alternative is one of the excellent twin 35 or 30 millimetre anti-air Oerlikon gun systems, firing at a rate of 1100 rounds a minute, compared with the Phalanx's 3000, but a less complicated and easier to maintain set-up that can be aimed visually or by radar. Another possibility being developed is the Sea Guard Contraves/Oerlikon 25 millimetre quick-firing cannon, coupled with the new Plessey Sea Guard radar, to give similar vital close-in protection.

In view of criticisms that have been levelled from time to time by politicians, the media, 'experts' and others about the Royal Navy's ships' design, it is clear that the performance of the frigates and destroyers, together with the supporting vessels, in the Falklands conflict was excellent. The weather was often appalling. The main base was 8000 miles away. Ships were constantly at sea and constantly subject to battle conditions with weapons firing and prolonged periods of high speed and high manoeuvrability. They proved reliable, strong, had good sea-keeping abilities and provided stable weapon and helicopter platforms. That they were well handled by highly competent seamen and engineers goes without saying. I have already referred to the design shortcomings that lack of finance imposed on the earlier Type 42 destroyers. Another factor that caused concern was the inflammability of ships.

I think that it is true to say that ships in all modern navies since the early 1960s have tried to provide better living conditions, attractive furniture and fittings and a pleasant, if sometimes plastic, decor for their crews, to whom the ship is a second home. This of course is a factor in retaining their services in a voluntary as opposed to conscripted force. However, if making a ship attractive to live in adds to the fire or splinter hazards when she is in action then the time has come to change this policy. As the Controller of the Navy, Vice Admiral Sir Lindsay Bryson, told engineering ratings at their training establishment in Gosport on 12th August 1982: 'Standards of comfort in warships must in future be reduced to improve their ability to survive in war.... various additions put into ships in the past to. improve accommodation standards would have to be removed so that there would be no repetition of what has happened in the last few months.'

Foam-filled furniture, whether the foam is plastic or rubber, will probably be eliminated. Steel springs do not generate smoke in the way a burning foam-filled mattress or cushion does. A very long hard look will need to be taken at all decorative fabrics, carpets, plastic, wooden or aluminium fittings. The Royal Navy is not of course alone in this. As Navy Minister I visited American, Canadian, Dutch, French, Italian and West German ships. To a greater or lesser extent they have the same problem. More fundamental is the use of materials in ships' structures. The modern ship is a mass of electrical cables and clearly their insulation covering should resist fire and also not give off choking smoke and fumes if subjected to a blaze. These are obviously matters of high priority for ships being built and I would expect to see these lessons taken into account at the refit of each existing ship and the consequent removal from it of unsuitable materials as soon as possible.

There is no question that the ships destroyed by bombs and

missiles all burned fiercely before they sank. One of the reasons, as far as *Sheffield* is concerned, may well have been unused rocket fuel ignited and blown around by the force of the impact. Another reason may have been the inflammability of the furnishings and other materials. A further factor which has received little mention, but I think is significant, concerns the type of fuel used in ships to drive their main engines.

Until the 1960s most major warships were powered by steam turbines, the steam being generated in large boilers which were mounted in a separate boiler room in the ship. These boilers were fired by a treacle-like substance called Furnace Fuel Oil or FFO. This was very viscous, had a very high flash point and indeed had to be heated before it could be ignited and sprayed into the fireboxes of boilers. Consequently it was a safe fuel to use as it was not a major fire hazard. If a ship sank and FFO floated on the water that was a different matter. It could do grave damage to lungs and internal organs if swallowed and indeed it is very similar to the crude oil that finds its way on to the world's beaches and does so much damage to sea birds.

With the advent of the gas turbine all this changed. Gas turbines run on a light, low viscosity fuel which has a low flash point and is much more inflammable than the old FFO. At the same time, just to confuse matters, existing ships were modernised so that their boilers could be fired by a similar, lighter fuel. FFO thus largely disappeared from the Royal Navy, although it is still used in HMS *Hermes* and the Royal Yacht *Britannia*.

The Type 21 and 22 frigates and Type 42 destroyers are all gas turbine powered, as are the 'Invincible' Class carriers, while the 'County' Class destroyers have a combination of gas turbine and conventional steam turbine propulsion. Thus the gas turbine fuel of the two Type 42 destroyers and two Type 21 frigates that were lost in the Falklands Campaign may well have been contributors to the fierce fires in them. However, in a gas turbine powered ship a boiler room and boilers are not needed, neither are high pressure steam lines snaking from the boiler room to the engine room to drive the turbines. I believe this had a significant effect upon casualties which, although each was a personal tragedy, overall were relatively small in numbers for the destruction of four ships. If an older type of ship suffered severe damage in her machinery spaces, there was a considerable chance of the boilers exploding or the steam lines rupturing, killing not only the substantial crew numbers in the boiler and engine rooms but many other people in the ship as well. I consider this factor was most important and the compartmentalised nature of modern ships, where groups of people work in spaces sealed off one from another, also helped significantly to limit loss of life. Finally, the skills of damage control training are well taught in the Royal Navy—the arts of first aid, fire fighting, ship stability, emergency lighting, power ventilation and repair (shoring up with wooden breasts to reinforce weakened bulkheads for instance). All these, under expert direction from a control headquarters, coupled with excellent discipline, undoubtedly saved lives and probably ships as well.

Unfortunately the same claim could not be made for the working overalls, made of synthetic material, which according to press reports did not give adequate protection against flash and burns. Some weeks after the loss of *Sheffield*, a number of whose survivors suffered serious burns, large numbers of overalls made of fire resistant treated cotton were flown to the forward base at Ascension Island and then transported by sea to the Task Force to replace those in service. Again I think this was not exclusively a Royal Navy problem but applied to a greater or lesser extent to all the services involved.

Incredibly, press reports have indicated that the Joint Services Clothing Research Centre at Colchester, Essex, has in the past refused fire retarding materials to be woven into fabric, because of their cost. This is another lesson to be learnt and acted upon swiftly. Cost should not be the deciding element in the provision of safe clothing.

Whilst I am discussing the unpleasant consequences of explosion and fire in ships, I ought to touch on the matter of aluminium in their construction. This was something seized upon by certain sections of the media, so that eventually people came to think that every Royal Naval ship was entirely made of aluminium and one spark would start a conflagration. The truth was somewhat different. The only Royal Navy ships with aluminium superstructure are the Type 21 frigates and the old 'ton' class minesweepers, where it was used in conjunction with wood because of its non-magnetic properties. Modern ship designers have to mount weapon systems, radar aerials, and masts well above the upper deck. These, together with the much lighter gas turbine engines, all pose stability problems that were not there in the older steam powered ships with their heavy boilers. In simple terms, the centre of gravity of the modern ship has moved higher and there is a danger that she will become top heavy. To counteract this, weight has to be saved, particularly on fittings above the waterline, and this has led to the increased use, throughout the world, not only of aluminium but also of fibre-glass, plastics and alloys of various kinds.

It is worth noting, by the way, that the *Q.E.2* has 1400 tonnes of aluminium in her superstructure and this is one reason why a vessel of 58,000 tons has the same passenger carrying capacity as the *Queen Elizabeth*, of 84,000 tons, which she replaced. *Canberra* and many other modern liners use aluminium extensively in the upper works and fittings. Many ships of the US Navy incorporate aluminium to a greater or lesser extent including the new *Aegis* guided missile cruiser and FFG frigates, while the Japanese destroyer escort, the *Islinkari*, has an aluminium superstructure to reduce weight. The same philosophy has been put into practice around the world since aluminium shows a fifty per cent weight saving over steel.

Back in 1972 an accidental missile explosion in the air over the USS *Warden*, a destroyer on duty in the Indian Ocean, shattered the ship's aluminium superstructure. Three years later, in 1975, the cruiser USS *Belknap* was damaged in a collision with the carrier USS *John F. Kennedy*. The resulting fire melted down the aluminium superstructure to the deck of the vessel. These incidents caused a considerable amount of research to take place and some shortcomings to be recognised.

First, it must be said that under normal conditions aluminium does not burn. This is blindingly obvious to every housewife with an aluminium saucepan and a gas ring. It softens and then melts at about 600 degrees Celsius, that is half the melting point of steel, but is still pretty hot. Heat of that intensity, however, can quickly be generated after a hit from a bomb or missile and thus the structure of a ship weakened before firefighting measures have a chance to be successful. The problems of fragmentation or splinter damage have been investigated by the United States Navy and their rule of thumb assessment is that a pound weight of aluminium in a given area will give the same protection as a pound weight of steel. However, the whole object of using aluminium is to save weight, so this is clearly not very satisfactory.

Following the *Belknap* fire the United States Navy carried out many tests and much research and seems to have found the right answer. The problems of melting temperatures are dealt with by fitting the aluminium structure with aluminium silicate cladding, which is a refractory insulation material. This is fitted retrospectively as ships go into dock for refit and 'fire protected zones' are created, all the aluminium being covered. This significantly delays the time the aluminium reaches its melting point in a conflagration, and gives the firefighters and damage control parties time to deal with the blaze and cool the structure down. Newly constructed ships will of course have this fitted whilst they are being built. The Americans estimate the cost of adding this insulation to the average existing ship with an aluminium superstructure to be about £2 millions.

The splinter protection problem is overcome by applying a laminate of 'Kevlar', which is a dense fire resistant synthetic fabric, to the heat insulating material in the areas where defence against fragmentation is particularly required. All this reduces the weight advantage of aluminium to steel by about five per cent, which is acceptable. There are obviously fittings like accommodation ladders which are better made of steel and no doubt the operational evaluation of the South Atlantic battle will look into these technical and detailed points. My own view is that the Americans seem to have solutions for the main problems. Certainly the ship designer has a formidable task in keeping weight down and making ships into stable platforms, unless he can use weight-saving materials like aluminium. Provided the technical experts take all the necessary steps to ensure that these can meet shortcomings of temperature and fragmentation, and I see no reason why they cannot, then I believe the Royal Navy should not discard this metal. There should, however, be a programme for the retrofitting of the Type 21 frigates with appropriate insulation and splinter protection where necessary.

In the days before the Royal Navy concentrated upon the North Atlantic and had forces all around the world, there were fleet repair and maintenance ships that provided much needed support for the ships' engineers. Rather like floating garages of a very sophisticated kind, they incorporated engineering workshops well equipped with machine tools, instrument repair shops and electronic test facilities. Those that acted as a 'mother ship' for submarines had good accommodation and baths aboard for the submariner to luxuriate in when his boat came alongside. Others provided similar facilities for destroyers or coastal forces. Some were purpose built, some were converted from merchant ships or old carriers. The last, HMS *Triumph*, a converted carrier dating back to the 1940s, in which as a young cadet from Dartmouth I witnessed my first carrier operations, was finally scrapped in 1981 because she was at the end of her useful life, having been in reserve at Chatham for some years.

The Falklands conflict immediately showed how vital such ships were to the fleet. Fortunately the *Stena Sea Speed*, a North Sea oil rig support ship of some 6000 tons, was requisitioned and converted to a repair ship rôle, with naval engineers to give technical back-up to its own crew. From all accounts the repair work carried out was first class, both to ships damaged by enemy action and to those damaged by the elements. In addition she provided good workshop facilities to keep things going when machinery broke down.

I believe two such ships based on the 'Stena' design and incorporating the lessons of the Falklands would be invaluable additions to the Royal Fleet Auxiliary. They would not only be valuable in their own right in future but would give useful experience of how best to deploy and use such ships in different situations; rather better than waiting for the next crisis to blow up, requisitioning civilian ships—if available—and learning the hard way.

The bigger ships like the carriers and assault ships do have a considerable 'in house' repair facility and *Invincible* must have created a record by changing one of her Rolls-Royce Olympus gas-turbine main engines while at sea off the Falklands in the middle of July 1982. These engines are a marine version of the engines that power the supersonic Concorde airliner. They weigh over three tons each and *Invincible* normally carries two spare engines on board. The particular engine to be replaced had exceeded its designed effective life and so, over a period of five days, a team of fourteen marine engineering mechanics removed the old engine and replaced it with a new one. To do this they had to move both engines up and down through several decks, in seas that were anything but smooth. The 'Invincible' Class ships, like the Type 22 frigates, have been designed so that engines can be changed without cutting away any of the surrounding structure or fittings. This again shows the flexibility of gas turbine power.

The operational and technical analyses of the Falklands conflict for the Navy, Army and Air Force will take a long time and the implementation of all the lessons learned and conclusions drawn will take much longer still. Clearly the campaign demonstrated that we need both guns and missiles, and neither are much use unless our early warning of approaching aircraft, missiles or ships is good. This means modern well tuned sets and aerial arrays in the ships. It means an organic airborne surveillance radar capability available twenty-four hours a day. This has to be part of the Fleet's equipment and the Fleet should not rely upon another service or another ally to provide it. The missiles and guns themselves should be up to date and deficiencies in performance must be removed in an evolutionary modernisation programme. The same philosophy and practice must be applied to naval electronic warfare equipment and electronic counter measures and 'chaff' devices which provide the ultimate protection for the ship against attacking missiles. This is a part of modern defence that is very much 'boffins' territory'. Our British scientists are as good as any in the world in this particular field. We have to make sure the fruits of their inventiveness are used, however, and not allowed to languish, since much more can be done to help merchant ships and fleet auxiliaries with passive defence of this kind.

A ship's designer obviously has to take into account the various conditions under which the ship and her crew will operate when he decides which materials to use. The maintenance and refitting cycle, the ship's projected rôle and the weapons and sensors she will carry all have to be taken into account. Since finance will always be tight, that parameter cannot be ignored. As I have tried to show, the Navy is already aware that the scales must be tilted back a bit towards fire resistance and serviceability and away from comfort and accommodation standards.

The most important criticism voiced by some commentators and whispered by others dubious of maritime power, concerns the vulnerability of surface ships. The Royal Navy lost two modern destroyers and two modern frigates to attacks by medium-technology jet aircraft, to say nothing of the virtual destruction of two Landing Ships, *Sir Lancelot* and *Sir Tristram*, and the loss of the

Atlantic Conveyor. Do not these losses prove how desperately vulnerable surface ships are and, by implication, what a waste of time and money the surface fleet is altogether? This is the argument put at its most extreme; paler shades of the same theme lay behind the philosophy of the 1981 Defence Review which proposed such dramatic cuts in the surface fleet. The question was well answered in part by Geoffrey Pattie, Under Secretary of State for Defence for Procurement, in the Royal Navy debate in Parliament on 19th July 1982, when he said:

> Although anyone can appreciate the basic rôle of the task force as the carrier of the troops and their supplies, the ships were also essential to the command, control and communications aspects of the battle. The ships gave essential fire support to troops going ashore and, by attacking the runways at Port Stanley. Ships provided protective screens against Argentine submarines and took a heavy toll of attacking aircraft. All of these factors have to be taken into account, because only surface ships could have carried out these tasks, and talk of them being 'vulnerable' as meaning 'susceptible of injury, not proof against weapon.'
>
> I should like to know what weapon system is not vulnerable in modern warfare. [20]

He could of course have gone on to say that the destruction of over one hundred Argentinian aircraft showed the vulnerability of that form of warfare, or that the reported loss also in July 1982 of one hundred Israeli tanks in her initial push into Lebanon against the PLO showed the vulnerability of tanks. It is not, of course, the losses in isolation that should be measured but what is achieved overall. The two Type 21 frigates *Ardent* and *Antelope* were lost in Falkland Sound because they limited their own freedom of action so that they could give anti-air, ground bombardment protection and support to the 5000 troops who landed ashore without a casualty and without losing one piece of equipment. It was a price that had to be paid and the big ships, including *Fearless, Intrepid* and *Canberra*, survived unscathed as a result. Similarly, as I have emphasised several times, better early warning radar and more Sea Harriers could well have saved *Sheffield* and *Coventry*.

The Falklands campaign was not a naval operation simply because of the long distance from the United Kingdom to those Islands. The weight and volume of stores required and the number of troops to be transported demanded surface forces to convey them and surface escort ships with the endurance to remain on station for months on end, and an ability to survive an Antarctic winter. To those who say the Falklands Conflict was a 'one off' operation I would reply that a winter war in the North Atlantic would be remarkably similar, except that the amount of stores, numbers of troops to be transported and ships to be escorted would be multiplied many times.

At the end of the day we cannot move large quantities of men and material across seas in submarines, as they are too small and too few, and are vulnerable to anti-submarine warfare forces. We cannot fly all the troops and stores because we shall never have enough aircraft, and anyway transport planes and their airfields, even assuming that we control them at both departure and destination, are vulnerable to attack. The only way to do it is with surface ships. Of course they are vulnerable to attack but, as I have shown, this vulnerability can be reduced if there is the right mix of high quality escorts. The South Atlantic War has highlighted a number of priorities for our future defence policy. I have left perhaps the most important of all these, the question of manpower, till last. I believe that the skill, professionalism, and character of the all-volunteer British Services were a most potent force in our victory in the Falklands. British servicemen had to face appalling conditions and they did so with courage and a blessed sense of humour.

After the conflict was over I was privileged to meet a number of my constituents who had served in the Royal Marines, the Army and the Royal Navy in the battle. They had fought a strange conflict: whilst they were facing death and seeing some of their friends killed or cruelly injured, life for their families and friends, even the majority of their Service colleagues, went on as normal. Although the two countries were at war it was possible, if unlikely, that England might have played Argentina in the World Cup Soccer Competition. British press, radio and television reporters were, with one or two unfortunate exceptions, more or less free to come and go and file their despatches in Buenos Aires. Argentinians in Britain enjoyed the same freedom, indeed I debated with one at the

Cambridge Union three weeks after the invasion.

The fact that these young servicemen came through their experience so well says a great deal for their characters, their training and the leadership they received from their NCOs and Officers. Having shown their true qualities and demonstrated that they at least are one part of contemporary British life which the world respects, it would be folly to undermine their morale and prestige by implementing the 1981 defence cuts which sought to make savings in equipment and men unrelated to the threat that faces us or the tasks we have to do.

This table shows the steady decline in carriers, conventional submarines, frigates and minesweepers over the sixteen years from 1966 to 1982, and a matching decline in their Royal Fleet Auxiliary support.

SHIPS OF THE ROYAL NAVY (Including ships on standby, modernising or refitting)

	April 1966	April 1976	April 1982
Aircraft Carriers	5	1	1
Commando Carriers	2	2	1
Assault Ships	2	2	2
Cruisers	5	2	-
Destroyers	20	9	12
Frigates	67	58	47
Mine Counter-Measures Vessels	97	40	34
Polaris submarines (SSBN)	-	4	4
Nuclear Hunter-Killer submarines (SSN)	2	8	11
Diesel/Electric submarines (SSK)	43	19	16
Royal Fleet Auxiliary (tankers and stores ships)	37	26	18
Royal Navy's Total Manpower (including WRNS)	98,000	69,000	65,000

Source: Ministry of Defence

10. Political Implications

When as a Minister I started to wrestle with the proposed Navy cuts in 1980 and more particularly 1981 I was constantly amazed that we run our country with almost a total lack of what business would call a 'corporate approach'. Notwithstanding the Cabinet and Permanent Secretary system and in spite of their close proximity, each of the great Departments of State amazingly goes its own separate way. Thus if the Ministry of Defence or Customs and Excise, for example, make redundant large numbers of people, it may or may not be in the national interest but that is not of major concern to them because the Department of Health and Social Security or the Department of Employment will pick up the revenue cost of unemployment benefit or retraining. This cost comes from a demand-set budget that has to be met, so the actual savings to the nation at the end of the day may be nil or even negative. Similarly if the Foreign Office want a particular ship or unit to carry out essential tasks as part of our foreign policy, HMS *Endurance* being a good case in point, then it has to be paid for out of their budget rather than from the defence budget.

I have already described the ludicrous situation concerning, for example, fishery protection, where the Royal Navy is treated like a kind of maritime 'Securicor'. An equally potty and long drawn out situation that seems to defy resolution has been the well publicised saga over whether the Ministry of Defence or the Department of Trade should pay the capital cost of much needed new survey ships. With less than one third of the United Kingdom continental shelf surveyed to modern standards the need for them has been urgent for a number of years, as Edward du Cann, Taunton's Member of Parliament and Chairman of the Conservative backbench committee, has pointed out in a series of telling parliamentary debates. The Navy has not enough money for 'warships', and so surveys have low priority in relation to defence needs. The Department of Trade argues correctly that the survey must be completed but has no

155

money with which to pay for it. It argues that the Hydrographic establishment at Taunton however comes under Navy control, and that the Hydrographer is an Admiral so the Ministry of Defence must pay. I believe that Naval ships and sailors are properly a charge on the Ministry of Defence, but their budget allocation should take 'civilian' tasks into account.

In an ideal world these nonsenses and misunderstandings would be sorted out by civil servants at various levels or by Ministers if really important decisions are to be taken. Unfortunately when budgets and manpower are being constantly squeezed and when senior civil servants and Ministers lead enormously pressurised lives, there never seems to be enough time to get a grip on this kind of problem. This Departmental insularity is not of course confined to the United Kingdom, nor I am sure, confined even to democracies. Indeed un-democratic states have even more cumbersome expensive bureaucracies. Nevertheless we suffer from it to an infuriating and sophisticated degree and when serious changes are being proposed in the different arms of defence or major upheavals are happening in the world's trade or economy then it does behove us to make sure that at least we define where our true interests lie and try to ensure that all the relevant Departments of State have policies that are heading more or less in the same direction.

So that, for example, if a skilled naval shipbuilding firm were to close because of a hiccup in naval orders, this will affect unemployment, regional policy, and export trade and a long term hard-won defence resource in the yard, with its equipment and its skilled teams, will be lost. It may well be cheaper in national financial terms and more sensible from the long-run strategic viewpoint to place orders to keep the yard going for ships which we need in any event.

Even if we have turned the British Empire into a Commonwealth, we do still have residual political, economic and particularly defence commitments some of which I have listed earlier. But we have major defence obligations also to all sorts of other national interests such as our merchant and fishing fleets, and our oil and gas industries. If we have political commitment to secure these various interests because it is very much to Britain's advantage to do so, then we must have the political determination to will the means to carry these policies out wherever and whenever needed. If we are not prepared to do this we should stop fooling ourselves and our allies and be honest enough to cut our various commitments and adopt a policy of 'sauve qui peut'. Whether such reneging will be sensible or politically acceptable to parliament is another matter.

Our key defence commitment is of course as part of the North Atlantic Treaty Organisation, an alliance that has preserved a sometimes fragile but nevertheless enduring peace in Western Europe for over thirty years. Unfortunately NATO has fifteen countries all 'doing their own thing' just like government departments.

Chauvinism in arms production, failure to meet agreed financial targets for overriding national reasons and just plain contrariness from disparate democracies cause the Alliance an enormous amount of wasted effort within its organisation. It is plagued by non-standardisation of arms, a lack of agreement over common specifications and much misdirected effort.

The threat from the Warsaw Pact does not diminish, and with the terrifying escalation in arms costs, it really is time that the Alliance made more substantial progress on common weapon systems with each country making its specific contribution to the partnership. Francis Pym, when Defence Secretary, floated the concept of 'Burden Sharing' at the NATO Defence Ministers' meeting in Brussels in December 1980. He called for greater specialisation by the various members of NATO in those things they did best, so that a fresh look could be taken at the tasks concerned and the various ways of fulfilling them. Unfortunately among the Ministers present the American team was in the process of change because of the new incoming Administration, the Dutch and later the Norwegians were to have elections and change their Ministers, while Francis Pym himself was to leave Defence three weeks after the Brussels meeting. Not much more therefore was heard of the idea until at the NATO Summit Meeting on 10th June 1982 Mrs Thatcher made an important policy speech that did not receive the publicity it deserved. Having given a clear and precise analysis of the defence problems facing the Alliance she went on to ask:

What scope is there for greater co-operation and closer collaboration between our forces and our defence industries? It may be that there are also some operational tasks which

157

some members of the Alliance can undertake more effectively than others who, in turn, could take on a bigger rôle elsewhere.

Later in her speech she referred to the 'out of area' dangers, the world-wide threat:

> Our fortunes are affected by developments outside the NATO treaty area—as Afghanistan reminded us so vividly. Our dependence on important oil supplies and raw materials means that we have a crucial interest in the maintenance of stability throughout the world.... We need to devise a strategy which exploits the assets which we each possess, whether political, economic, commercial or military.... it does require a recognition that our security no longer lies simply in the defence of European territory but also in defence of our wider interests the world over. We must assure this by using all the means available to us whether jointly or separately. So shall we each enhance the security of all.

With all this I find myself in total accord. If these words are translated into action it means that countries must contribute to the Alliance their particular expertise, in many cases long established by history, geography, tradition and necessity. It also means not being mesmerised, to the exclusion of all else, by NATO and Warsaw Pact countries facing each other on the central plains of Europe. Thus I would argue that in Britain's case this would mean much greater emphasis on her maritime power both within and without NATO. Greater emphasis too with the Dutch on amphibious warfare and our combined Royal Marines/Netherlands Marine Corps that already work together very closely. The Germans and the Belgians would have perhaps a more important land rôle to play, particularly with their expertise in armoured warfare. Other examples within the Alliance could readily be drawn.

This does not mean the scrapping of the British Army of the Rhine to pay for a huge new Navy—far from it. But neither does it mean cutting the Navy's surface ships, their manpower, their logistic support to dangerous levels in order to preserve, apparently for ever, 55,000 soldiers in Northern Germany (with their ever increasingly expensive back-up and family support) because these numbers appeared sensible in the early 1950s. The cost to the British tax-payer, largely in Deutschmarks, of merely supporting our forces in Germany, not paying for the troops' wages or for their equipment, is estimated to be £788 millions in the financial year 1982/83 according to the 1982 Defence White Paper. This includes the employment of over 24,000 locally engaged German staff to help provide services. To put these figures into perspective the total cost of completed work in the five Royal Dockyards for the year 1980/81, including all labour, materials, services, administration and overheads, was £445 millions, and the total number of United Kingdom personnel working in the dockyards in 1982 was about 29,000; this was of course before the proposed closure of Chatham and Gibraltar and the major rundown of Portsmouth.

It may be that family and social support for a constant number of British Servicemen is of importance not only to the German economy but also to our political policies in Europe and our defence policies as a member of NATO. I for one doubt very much however that it is of greater importance than a devastating reduction in our maritime power. Nor do I believe that NATO is so fragile that the decrease of British troops on its Central Front or the reduction of their support facilities (especially if we increase our Atlantic and world-wide naval rôle) are subjects too sensitive for discussion.

It is worth remembering that in cost benefit terms, the United Kingdom provides seventy per cent of NATO's Eastern Atlantic (i.e. maritime) Forces at a cost of twenty-three per cent of the U.K. Defence Budget. This compares with our provision of ten per cent of the Allied Forces in the Central Region of Europe for some forty-one per cent of our Defence budget. I believe that it is in NATO's interests that the ideas floated by Francis Pym and given form and substance by the Prime Minister should be turned into a programme for action over a period of years. This, as far as the United Kingdom is concerned, means reversing the rundown of the Royal Navy and amphibious forces and taking a critical look at B.A.O.R. levels and their support costs in Germany with a view to achieving significant money savings.

Before we leave entirely the 'burden sharing' concept, mention must be made of Japan which has made a dramatic success of building up its economy since World War II. Japan relies heavily upon imported oil and other raw materials to keep her industrial momentum going. In 1980 for example, she received from the Middle East over 176 million tonnes of oil which was carried in twelve per cent of all the world's tanker voyages made that year. The protection of these tankers and other ships plying the world for the Japanese is largely undertaken by the United States Navy, the French Navy and the Royal Navy with their standing patrols around the Persian Gulf and North Indian Ocean. Nearer home the United States Pacific Fleet makes a significant contribution to stability in the area and to the safe and timely arrival of Japanese ships.

Japan for many years has spent less than one per cent of its Gross Domestic Product on defence compared with Britain's near five per cent and the United States' seven per cent. Thus the tax burden of Japanese industries does not have to reflect the heavy proportion of defence costs that American or British firms have to pay. This is an interesting thought on which the American and British taxpayers might ponder as they drive around in their Datsuns, watch their Sanyo televisions and click away with their Yashica cameras! During a visit to Tokyo in the spring of 1982 Caspar Weinberger, the American Defense Secretary, said 'expansion and modernisation of [Japanese] forces remains insufficient in view of the need for a greater sharing of America's military burden in Asia'. [21] The problems, according to the Japanese Government, are the various treaties made after the war and particularly the views of the Japanese people who are, many of them, very much opposed to any resurgence of Japanese 'militarism'. Where defence expansion has taken place I have noticed a robust determination by the Japanese to develop and fit as much of their own equipment as possible, a determination that I admire and one that is perhaps rivalled only by the French. A few individual British firms like Rolls-Royce have gained valuable contracts to supply engines for the ships of the Japanese maritime defence force.

However if Japan, for political reasons, is unable to substantially expand and modernize its forces it should be possible to devise a formula whereby the efforts made by the United States, Britain and France, in particular, to provide maritime protection are recognised by some form of off-set payment, either in cash terms or by the placing of research, development and production contracts in these three countries. As the balance of trade between the countries favours Japan there will be more and more pressure for it to make a contribution towards the defence costs of its allies whose efforts make secure the maritime trade upon which Japan depends.

It is clear that whatever economies may be made in the Navy, the British Army of the Rhine, the Ministry of Defence in the administrative staff or elsewhere, it yearly becomes more and more difficult to maintain well paid, well equipped all-volunteer forces to meet Britain's various commitments. The annual three per cent increase in defence expenditure, which has not quite been achieved in the years 1979-82, is clearly inadequate, not least because the defence equipment inflation is several points higher than ordinary inflation. To take account of this and other factors probably means an increase of nearer five per cent, allowing for inflation, which in 1982 would have meant about £300 millions more for the Defence budget. I believe that the Falklands Conflict has shown the penalties of inadequate weapons or sensors to meet current threats from potential enemies and that the British public would accept the extremely modest increase in taxation required to provide for adequate conventional arms.

It is clear that even if NATO can devise a better system in line with Mr Pym's and Mrs Thatcher's suggestions, even if the Japanese play a rather fuller financial part either by arms purchases or by some other means in the defence of the free world, even if the British and other Western economies start to grow again on a steady and sustained basis as I believe they will, there are going to be for the United Kingdom major resource restraints, constantly limiting what can be done for defence. At the moment the strategic nuclear deterrent is costing annually between one and two per cent of the defence budget. A brand new sophisticated system will cost a very great deal more and will, inevitably, compound the difficulties of too few resources chasing too many tasks across the services.

Thus it was on the morning of 15th July 1980 I was attending a special service to celebrate the 350th anniversary of the founding of Norton Knatchbull School in Ashford, Kent. That afternoon the Prince of Wales was to join parents and staff at the school and it promised to be an interesting and happy day. As I left the church a Police Inspector apologetically took me to one side and asked me to ring the Ministry straight away. Controlled pandemonium greeted me there; a press leak in the United States was obliging the

Secretary of State to make a statement to Parliament that afternoon on the Government's decision to purchase the Trident Nuclear ballistic missile system from America. Would I join him on the Front Bench in the House of Commons? I made my quick but sincere apologies to the School and arrived alongside Francis Pym in time for the Parliamentary statement. The actual decision had been taken by a small group within the Cabinet and I had not been involved but it seemed to me, on the available evidence, that this was the right decision to take. Our present strategic nuclear deterrent, the submarine-launched Polaris missile, would be obsolete in the mid 1990s and the four special nuclear-powered submarines would be too old and too noisy by then. The operational life of Polaris was being extended to the 1990s by fitting its warheads with a device called 'Chevaline' which had cost £1000 millions to develop and which enabled the warheads to evade being hit and destroyed by enemy defending missiles.

The estimated cost of Trident, including the submarines and support facilities based on the Trident missile, was £4500-£5000 millions; this cost would of course be spread over fifteen years and would be funded, as I understood, by the defence budget as a whole in the same way as the present Polaris system. The Royal Navy would continue to specifically fund the revenue costs of the system when it was operational. In the exchange of letters between the Prime Minister and President Carter, Mrs Thatcher made it clear that the purchase of Trident should not in any way prejudice our conventional forces, indeed quite the reverse; in paragraph four of her letter of the 10th July 1980, she wrote:

> In particular I would like to assure you that the United Kingdom Government continues to give whole-hearted support to the NATO Long Term Defence Programme and to other strengthening of conventional forces ... the objective of the United Kingdom Government is to take advantage of the economies made possible by the co-operation of the United States in making the Trident I missile system available in order to reinforce its efforts to upgrade its conventional forces. [22]

President Carter, in his letter of reply dated 14th July said: 'I view as important your statements that the Polaris successor force will be assigned to NATO and that your objective is to take advantage of the economies made possible by our co-operation to reinforce your efforts to upgrade the United Kingdom's conventional forces. As you know I regard the strengthening of NATO's conventional and nuclear forces as of highest priority for Western security.' [23]

A number of problems fairly quickly started to develop. On the American side it became clear that they were thinking seriously about the phased reduction of the Trident I missile and its replacement with the larger, more powerful and more accurate Trident II. When I visited the United States in March 1981 this was one of the areas for discussion. No firm decision had been taken at that time but I returned convinced that the United States would develop Trident II and make an announcement within twelve months. In fact the announcement came in October 1981 that the US Navy was switching to Trident II missiles with a view to deploying them at sea by 1989.

On the British side the failure of our economy to grow at the expected rate, coupled with increasing financial pressures on the Defence budget, made a number of people, who were by no means inclined to the viewpoint of nuclear disarmament, question the wisdom of pre-empting such a large amount of money for what was essentially not only a political weapon system but a gold-plated one at that. I was always a supporter of Trident because I believed that Britain should have its own long-range nuclear weapon capability rather than rely entirely upon the United States for it. However, my support was always based on the premise that it was a national strategic system and that its capital cost would be so funded, otherwise the effect upon the budget of the particular service providing the launching platform, be it Navy or Air Force, could be calamitous.

The American decision to go for Trident II meant that we really had to follow suit. On the time scale envisaged by the US Navy it looked as if, by the time our Trident I submarines were entering service in the mid 1990s, the Americans would be withdrawing the last of their Trident I missiles from service. We would therefore be the sole operators of Trident I, if that was our choice, and the cost and problems of operating a unique system from scratch would be very large. Accordingly, in March 1982, Mr Nott announced that the Government had chosen the Trident II system as their operational service, and that the logistic support could then be on the same time scale as that of the Americans. He also said that the Trident force would consist of four large new submarines each armed with sixteen missiles. The total cost of the new system, allowing for inflation, the drop in the value of the pound and the more expensive missiles, had increased from about £4500 millions to £7500 millions at September 1981 prices. Since that date, costs have risen further, the dollar has strengthened against the pound and the September 1982 figure of cost is likely to be nearer £8500 millions. There are many who believe the true figure will turn out higher still.

Mr Nott's announcement on 9th September 1982 that all the maintenance and servicing of the missiles would be carried out at the US Trident base in Kings Bay, Georgia, made logistic and financial sense. However, it means that several thousand jobs will not be created in Scotland with the abandonment of the proposed facilities at Coulport. It does also raise in many people's minds very real doubts about how independent British Trident will really be. This could be particularly true of the perception, no matter how wrong, from Moscow.

It had become clear in 1981, notwithstanding a smoke-screen from the Ministry of Defence, that the major cost for the whole project was to be met by the Royal Navy. In his lecture to the Royal United Services Institution on 9th June 1982, the First Sea Lord confirmed this when he said: 'The Royal Navy was ... being saddled with virtually the whole of the bill for Trident.' Thus, although the Ministry quite correctly said that expenditure on Trident in the peak years, towards the end of the 1980s, would not exceed twelve per cent of the total defence equipment budget they did not comment on the fact that this would be nearly thirty per cent of the Royal Navy's equipment budget. In other words conventional ships and weapons will be foregone to accommodate this huge chunk of Trident expenditure.

Speaking to the Young Conservatives' National Conference in Harrogate on 13th February 1982 John Nott said: 'We spend a very small percentage of our defence budget on our nuclear forces. There are those who still ask whether it would not be better to devote those resources to our conventional forces. Of course we need tanks and ships and aircraft too, but which would the Soviet Union rather we had? A few extra British tanks to add to our 650—when they have 50,000 of them—or Trident? A few extra British ships or aircraft, or

Trident? You only have to ask the question to know the answer.'

As I am sure Mr Nott knows, the capital cost of Trident would buy twenty-four 'Invincible' Class aircraft carriers, or ninety new Type 23 frigates—more than trebling our frigate force. I do not therefore share the Defence Secretary's strong conviction that Admiral Gorshkov would rather that Britain trebled its frigate force or increased the 'Invincible' Class eightfold instead of having one, or at the most two, Trident submarines on patrol as an addition to the United States' fifteen or so large 'Ohio' Class submarines each carrying twenty-four of these missiles.

My growing concern about the way Trident was to be funded, coupled with the problems of national economic growth that were not going to be solved quickly, caused my support for the project to wane, and I searched for a weapon system that could be a credible British deterrent but need not cost the earth or raise so many political problems. By 1982 there were many people in all parties who in no way had CND beliefs or were of pacifist views but who had major doubts about, if not outright hostility to, the effect which the cost of Trident could have on our conventional forces.

At the end of 1981 I had detailed non-classified discussions with some of the executives of the General Dynamics Corporation who make the Tomahawk cruise missile. This in its ground-launched version is the medium-range weapon to be stationed in Britain, Italy and other NATO countries as part of NATO's modernisation of 'theatre' nuclear weapons. However it was the submarine launched version that interested me. Tomahawk flies at a height of about 100 feet and is capable of various ranges from 250 to 1750 miles depending on its mission. Its speed is 500 miles an hour and it can be armed with a nuclear warhead or conventional high explosive. Much development work is still going on and the latest advance, I was told, was to fit Tomahawk into vertical launchers in surface ships or submarines. The US Navy is first of all employing shorter range conventionally armed Tomahawks in its nuclear hunter/killer submarines. With vertical launchers twelve or twenty-four can be carried in a submarine together with its full complement of torpedoes fired in the normal way through tubes.

If Tomahawk with a nuclear warhead and a range of 2000 miles flying at supersonic speeds could be developed, this might well be a credible long-range deterrent for Britain. They could be fitted to our

165

new conventional submarines and our existing hunter/killer nuclear class could be adapted to take vertical launchers, or they could be fired like the medium-range missile Sub-Harpoon out of the existing torpedo tubes. There would be nothing to stop us having vertical launchers of thirty-six or more missiles in a suitably designed surface ship. These would be easier to stop, possibly, than the multiple warheads of Trident, but the Soviets would not know which of our nuclear and conventional submarines at any time was carrying such missiles, it could be any of twenty-odd boats on patrol compared with a maximum of two Trident boats. Since Polaris will remain effective for another thirteen years or so it seemed to me and to those I spoke to at General Dynamics, that during this time cruise missile technology will make a quantum jump to produce the performance that we require. I should point out that General Dynamics Corporation own the Electric Boat Company of Groton, Connecticut, which makes the Trident submarines for the US Navy so they have no axe to grind in agreeing with me.

Taking this whole concept a stage further I and my friend and parliamentary colleague Philip Goodhart MP, a former Army Minister, argued in the press and in the House of Commons that, if NATO's modernised 'theatre' nuclear weapons were sea launched from US Navy, Royal Navy and possibly Royal Netherlands Navy and Italian Navy submarines, much of the political hostility that has been manifest against ground-launched cruise missiles would disappear. It may be exasperating but it is understandable that people do not like nuclear missile launching bases in their neighbourhood! Put them out of sight under the sea and the problem, if it does not totally go away, does diminish. In all fairness we did not convince our Conservative colleagues, but that was before the Falklands invasion and before fresh thinking about defence was forced upon us all.

It certainly appeared from my discussions with General Dynamics that, although there were problems in developing Tomahawk, these would be overcome and there would soon be a new developing generation of advanced cruise missiles that could meet our political requirements in the time scale required. It also appeared that the cost, including that of adapting existing submarines, would be substantially less, perhaps fifty per cent less, than that of Trident. I guessed, although the company was far too discreet to confirm or deny it, that there had been little contact between the

Ministry and them about cruise missiles. I believe that the political, financial and defence issues involved are so important that a full appraisal of existing missiles and projected developments ought to be made before too much money is committed to Trident. I also believe that, if we proceed with Trident, the proposed method of funding—saddling the Royal Navy with virtually the whole cost is most unfair and really not sensible for it—means that the project will attract the added hostility and criticism of an influential section of the public, those who wish to see the United Kingdom adequately protected, but not at the expense of our maritime power.

There is always a danger that in highlighting the massive maritime and military might of the Soviet Union and its allies we may exaggerate the Soviets' other strengths and endue them with powers and qualities that they do not possess. While it is always folly to underestimate a potential adversary, it can be very foolish to accept him at his own propaganda value. In the Western democracies free speech is a precious asset and there will always be those who, for a variety of motives ranging from gullibility to venality, will question the build-up in Western forces, will always seek to justify Soviet military might at whatever level, and will, from their safe comfortable capitalist havens, praise all things connected with the Soviet system. It is worth reminding our fellow citizens that one of the main reasons why the Soviet Union and the Warsaw Pact allies have built up such massive armies, airforces and global fleets is because of the failure of the ideology and practice of Communism to persuade people to join their cause. The emigration restrictions in the Soviet Union, the Berlin Wall, the minefields on the East German border are there to keep people in, not to keep the West out. There is nothing to stop the entire Royal Ballet leaving Britain tomorrow and settling to live and work in Moscow should they wish to do so. Yet every time the Bolshoi Ballet goes on tour some of their brightest young dancers seek political asylum in a country of the West since the individual is denied free choice.

The economies of Europe and North America have had a pretty lean two or three years in the late 1970s and early 1980s, but those of the Soviet Union have fallen far behind their planned targets with the sole exception of natural gas production. Economic growth rates, agriculture, coal and oil production, industrial productivity all have been unsatisfactory and have not reached the levels set in the various

167

five year plans. In recent years Russia's grain imports have varied between fifteen and thirty million tonnes, compared with an average of three million tonnes in the 1960s, while her nuclear-powered electricity generating capacity planned for 1980 was missed by a shortfall of sixty-six per cent. So the story, and the figures, could go on.

Yet military expenditure continues to run at about fourteen per cent of gross domestic product and this understates the true position, because many of the soldiers, sailors and airmen are conscripts and poorly paid. Labour costs of the Soviet Armed Forces are much lower in both relative and absolute terms than their British or American all-volunteer counterparts, so more money is available for high technology weapons and delivery systems. The problem for the Soviets of course is sustaining this, and at the same time giving a reasonable rise in living standards to their own people, together with providing the necessary investment in consumer-orientated production. It is interesting to note that the number of Muslims in the Soviet Union has risen from 27 millions in 1959 to 50 millions in 1982. With the growing unrest in the Muslim world this could pose considerable internal security problems in the future. We can also understand why Moscow has, during 1981 and 1982, ensured that the Polish Government has cracked down on the free Trade Union Movement 'Solidarity': the last thing the Soviet Government wants is the contagion of consumer politics and independent trade unions to spread throughout their East European satellites and perhaps fatally infect the USSR itself. That is why in 1981 a major joint-forces exercise named 'Zopod 81' took place under naval overall command. This amphibious exercise, which included a major landing on a site only a few miles outside the Polish Border, received heavy coverage on Warsaw Pact countries' television and in their newspapers. It involved the largest grouping of warships in the Baltic since World War II, including aircraft carriers, helicopter cruisers and the amphibious assault ship *Ivan Rogov* together with literally hundreds of other warships, hovercraft, merchant ships and landing craft. The object was political: to show the Poles and other weaker brethren in the Warsaw Pact what they could expect if they pushed resistance to Soviet type Communism too far. A secondary but important objective was to test plans for amphibious operations in distant areas.

Thus there are two forces pulling on the Soviet system. On the one side their real economic problems are likely to make military expansion, at the rate we have seen in recent years, impossible if living standards are to improve to any marked degree at the same time. On the other they have the powerful need to project their ideologies throughout the world and provide for massive offensive and defensive power against attacks from within or without the Warsaw Pact. How all these particular circles can be squared I do not know. But the Politbureau, who formulate the policy, seem to appreciate that a maritime package can bring economic advantage. The many facets of the Soviet Navy: the merchant and fishing fleets, the many vessels for oceanography and seabed mining and the huge naval fleets themselves would be effective against all enemies except those from a popular uprising from within the USSR itself. Even if defence expenditure is substantially reduced in the latter part of the 1980s Soviet maritime influence is now immense and almost self-sustaining.

The Soviet naval procurement machine is centralised, large, no doubt bureaucratic, certainly costly at the expense of the hapless Soviet consumer and directed with singlemindedness by Admiral Gorshkov. It works in that, unceasingly, ships, aircraft, weapons, and sensors of high quality appear in ever increasing numbers. In the United Kingdom weapons and equipment of high quality do appear, though never in sufficient numbers. But I have suspected it is in spite of rather than because of the systems we have created. In a nutshell there are too many complex committees before orders are placed and the Ministry of Defence itself is now too large and unwieldy. In contrast to the Soviet system I believe many of the problems stem from a very right and proper parliamentary account-ability of public money.

Back in 1964 the public accounts committee found that Ferranti had made 'excessive' profits on missile contracts being procured by the Ministry of Supply for the Ministry of Defence. Some tens of millions of pounds were involved and the company repaid some of this money. The event in itself was a minor *cause célèbre* but after the Left-wing politicians had scored some predictable points it died down. However its effects linger on apparently for ever: These days there is a body within the Ministry of Defence called the Procurement Executive which does the Services' purchasing, but because

169

everyone seems terrified of another Ferranti episode the amount of checking and double checking that takes place has to be seen to be believed.

Whilst I was visiting Westlands Helicopters factory at Yeovil in 1980, I was looking at a finished aircraft with Lord Aldington, the Chairman, and Basil Blackwell, the Chief Executive, when we noticed a sizeable crowd of people clustered round a new Lynx helicopter which had just been built. I asked who they were and what excited their interest and was told that three were Westlands engineers, the other twelve were from the Ministry; the object of their concern was a small light bulb fitting in the cockpit! Unfortunately this sort of story was to be repeated time and time again at all the factories of the Ministry's suppliers that I saw. Large numbers of Ministry personnel were constantly obliged to visit for comparatively unimportant matters. I did not blame the people concerned. The system was wrong, nobody was encouraged to unilaterally commit themselves to anything, they had to check and cross check and the cost in terms of time, travel and subsistence was horrendous. I know all the arguments about the possible misuse of public money and the fear that some industry is just waiting to take the Ministry 'to the cleaners' but I believe such anxiety is largely groundless. A few broad checks would soon establish the integrity of a supplier who, after all, has it in his own interests to keep his contract with the MOD.

Steps were being taken to try to inject some sense into this situation but during my last months as Navy Minister procurement problems were notorious. It seemed to me that nothing could be designed, much less ordered or produced, until the idea, the requirement, the concept, the project-definition and all the other in-words for the pre-design stages, had been tossed backwards and forwards by a plethora of bizarrely named committees. The upshot of all this barren activity seemed to be to delay the ship, tank, aeroplane, missile or whatever by two or three years and to escalate the cost in direct proportion to the number of committees that the project went through. I never cease to be impressed with the Dutch and the French, on the other hand, who can produce good equipment in a shorter time span with only minimal involvement by government staff. However, things were starting to improve in 1981 and I can only hope the momentum is maintained. It could hardly have become worse.

Political Implications

So we are back where this chapter opened. The lack of a corporate approach and a dearth of modern techniques mean that the Ministry of Defence is not run as efficiently as it might be and it is very big business. In 1982 it had a total budget of over £14,000 millions and it employed over 321,000 Service Personnel and over 243,000 civilian staff. It spent over £100 millions a year with each of eight major British firms and over £25 millions each with another eleven.

The Ministry of Defence was founded in 1963 by the merger of the old Admiralty, the Air Ministry, the War Ministry and the Defence Ministry at a time when such mergers were fashionable. The amalgamation of several car industries to form British Leyland came in 1968, and the Department of the Environment was formed from the Ministry of Housing and Local Government, Public Building and Works, and the Ministry of Transport in 1970. In the same year the Department of Trade and Industry grew out of the Board of Trade and the Ministry of Technology.

Now some ten years later British Leyland has been re-organised and has lost some of its constituent parts, the Department of the Environment has lost Transport and the Department of Trade and Industry has become a separate Department of Trade and a separate Department of Industry, with a special Minister for Information Technology. Only Defence has bucked the trend and has more power concentrated in fewer hands at the centre of a very large conglomerate organisation. As a Tory I have always been philosophically antipathetic to large Ministries and too much centralised control. Although within the Ministry of Defence there are many good people working hard at all levels to make the system more effective, nothing I saw in this large organisation altered my view.

11. What Kind of Navy Do We Need?

The Royal Navy in the sense of a permanent professional force of seamen, officers and ratings paid by the Crown came into existence only in the reign of Charles II. However, for hundreds of years before, merchant seamen like Drake and Frobisher had been commissioned into the service of their Sovereign long before the establishment of the British Empire. There is nowhere in Britain more than a hundred miles from the sea, and we have traded abroad and fished around our coasts for centuries; everything too, that was imported or exported, until about sixty years ago, had to travel by sea, and even today a vast proportion still does, and it is therefore not surprising that our history is inextricably involved with our maritime traditions.

It is a Tory axiom, and one practised with skill and enthusiasm by Margaret Thatcher as Prime Minister, that Government should not go against the grain of commonsense, of basic home truths, of national feelings. Most British people have a well-developed sense of fair play, coupled with a strong but normally dormant patriotism. That is why Margaret Thatcher and the Government by their swift and decisive action to recapture the Falklands by force, if negotiations failed, received the overwhelming backing of the country.

Most British people whether they live in Meriden in the heart of England, Manchester or Medway have a deep gut feeling that we need a strong Royal Navy and Merchant Fleet to look after Britain's interests and its trade. It is not just a question of joining in 'Rule Britannia' on the last night of the Promenade Concerts in the Albert Hall. It is an understanding that our history, experience and skills mean that we are far more than just the inhabitants of a series of islands off the coast of North West Europe. It is a recognition that we have world-wide responsibilities to our allies and to our own mercantile interests. I believe that to inhibit these feelings and to seek to reduce the maritime traditions which put them into practice is contrary to Conservative precepts.

The twelve months from Spring 1981 to Spring 1982 revealed a strange dichotomy in Conservative Government thinking. The 'cost accountant' philosophy which lay behind the substantial Royal Navy cuts of 1981, was quickly dead and buried when the crisis began and virtually no price was too high to achieve victory in the South Atlantic. Now of course the British forces which need to remain in the Falklands for their defence in the foreseeable future are clearly much greater than would have been deemed sufficient before April 1982. When a Tory Government passes 'O' level economics but fails 'A' level history it gets into trouble.

Since the 1981 cuts were announced (and vigorously defended) second and third thoughts have been brought to bear—some prompted by the Falklands crisis, others by perhaps a better understanding of what the implications would be. As a result the Amphibious Warfare Ships *Fearless* and *Intrepid* due for premature disposal were reinstated in February 1982. In April, as the Argentinian invasion was being mounted, a reprieve was announced for *Endurance* which would remain in service for many years to come on her South Atlantic duties. During the Conflict, the Type 12 frigates *Berwick*, *Rhyl* and *Falmouth* plus the Type 81 frigates *Gurkha*, *Tartar* and *Zulu* were all taken off the disposal list (they were due to be scrapped or sold), hastily refitted by the dockyards and all recommissioned in the fleet by the end of July. In the Defence debate that took place in Parliament, also in July, John Nott announced the reprieve from 'premature disposal' of the destroyers *Bristol*, *Glamorgan* and *Fyfe*. Things were beginning to look up!

They looked up even more when rumours that had been circulating for some time were finally confirmed and the Defence Secretary told Parliament in July that *Invincible* was not now to be sold to Australia as it had been decided that we did indeed need three carriers to keep two operational ... My own personal campaign, with others, for *Endurance* and *Invincible* had at last borne fruit, and this with the saving of the frigates and destroyers, plus the ordering of a further Type 22 frigate, was a big reversal of the nonsenses of summer 1981. Clearly too, Portsmouth dockyard was not going to be run down to the extent that had been planned, although Chatham and Gibraltar dockyards still seemed doomed. Various sources talk now about the possibility of fitting light-weight

Sea Wolf missile systems to ships so it appears that the policy of non-modernisation of ships is also to be quietly dropped. A lot of decisions still remained to be taken and the orders made to replace the two destroyers, two frigates and the two landing ships lost in the campaign.

The certainty that a large number of 'condemned' ships are now to be kept plus the promise that ships lost in action are to be replaced make the threat of the loss of 10,000 servicemen by 1986 look pretty silly. If these manpower reductions were to be carried out there would be insufficient sailors to man the increased level of ships. All these and other matters are being re-evaluated by the Ministry of Defence in the light of lessons learnt from the Falklands conflict. Whether Mr Nott's statement in the *Times* on 27th July 1982—'I believe that cool and reasoned analysis will show that the broad strategic decisions, which we took last year will produce the best balanced and most effective force structure to meet the prime threat from the Soviet Union and its allies into the 1990s and beyond'—is an understandable post-Falklands reaction to preserve his *amour propre* only time will show. I would contend that the changes in Navy policy already announced when Mr Nott wrote those words were a most significant shift from the 'broad strategic decisions' taken last year.

An analysis of the dangers facing this country and the tasks they imply for the Royal Navy indicates for us what maritime forces we require and enables us to assess their priority with competing claims from other services and other government departments. In Chapter Two I described in some detail the burgeoning Soviet naval threat which is now mounted on a world-wide basis. The Soviet Air Forces and Armies also contain daunting numbers although their lack of flexibility does not give them the world-wide presence that Gorshkov's Navy possesses or such an immediate power projection in the 'no peace no war' situation which we have lived with for many years. From the Royal Navy's viewpoint the Soviet threat is met on a number of levels all working within the NATO framework.

The Navy first of all is the provider of the United Kingdom's submarine-launched strategic nuclear deterrent currently operated by four nuclear powered submarines each carrying sixteen Polaris 2500 mile range missiles fitted with three separate warheads. This force is important politically but is not part of our maritime capability in the historic sense of that term; in the past our strategic nuclear force has comprised aircraft carrying air-launched weapons. The advantage of the nuclear submarine is its great endurance, its wide range of operational area in the seas and oceans that lie within a 2500 mile range of the planned targets and its comparative invulnerability to detection and destruction. For this force to operate efficiently, however, it does rely upon more conventional naval vessels like hydrographic surveying ships to chart the deep under-water passages for the submarines, while minesweepers and mine-hunters are vital to keep open the access routes for submarines going on and off patrol. These submarines are normally assigned to NATO and only in the most extreme and unlikely circumstances, if our vital interests were to be threatened, would we use them independently, but we do retain that right.

The second important task for the Navy is the traditional maritime one, control of the seas. In a NATO context that means control, with our allies, of the North Atlantic and Norwegian Sea. We have to provide the defence against the Soviet forces which can threaten NATO's Northern flank and vital ports and air bases in Northern Norway. This includes positive action through and to the East of Greenland-Iceland-UK-Norway gap to stop massive Soviet submarine or surface fleet incursion into the Atlantic, assuming we have enough notice. It also embraces the vital reinforcement and resupply shipping protection across the Atlantic and across the English Channel and the North Sea.

Assuming that any kind of conflict is not over in a few days, this task is fundamental to military success in Europe and envisages up to six hundred merchant ships being used in the Atlantic in the first month and needing protection from the airborne and underwater threats. The Soviets could put a mix of up to two hundred conventional and nuclear-powered submarines into the Atlantic and they would be unlikely to wait until the conflict had started before seeking to place them there. Thus anti-submarine warfare would be widespread and we would need to be on the offensive right from the start.

An additional high priority would be the escorting of the American Carrier Battle Groups in the North Atlantic when hostilities got under way. These big carriers with their in-depth air, missile and anti-submarine protection are likely to be less vulnerable

175

to destruction than the Allied fixed land bases whose positions are no doubt already on the target co-ordinates of the computers of the Soviet supersonic 'Backfire' bombers.

Reinforcements have to be landed and the protection against air, surface and sub-surface attack and mines in European coastal waters is another necessary adjunct to the protection of ships in the Atlantic. At the same time the Royal Marines and the Netherlands Marines have a primary task to reinforce and defend NATO's northern flank in North Norway. Though a certain amount of equipment is pre-positioned there for use in times of tension or conflict much will fall upon the not too broad shoulders of the Royal Navy.

We should not however make the mistake of thinking that the Soviet threat to the West starts on the plains of Central Germany and may possibly reach up to the North Cape, or down to Ankara, and that we can ignore anything beyond this axis. Since I do not believe that the Kremlin wants a nuclear holocaust any more than Whitehall or the Pentagon, the Soviets can achieve much by probing the West's weaknesses wherever they are to be found and this is a real and constant threat that we face day by day. By using a combination of armed might, economic power, and political pressure sometimes with surrogate states in the lead, the Soviets wish to spread their influence and ideology around the world, and they use their naval, merchant and fishing fleets as major forces to do this.

The very flexibility of maritime power enables the challenge to be met and blocked if we and our allies are determined. We need, however, sufficient ships 'out of area' if we are to ensure that the West's interests are protected and safeguarded. We must also have enough ships to protect the 'choke points' around the world, to see that important raw materials continue to reach our industries and to make sure that our merchant ships can go about their business without threats or disruptions.

There are many national rôles for the Royal Navy in which our allies are not normally involved at all. Fishery protection and the patrolling of our offshore oil and gas rigs are of growing importance, while the new 200-mile Exclusive Economic Zones (territories of sea up to 200 miles from a coastline where a nation has the right to the economic benefits from activities carried out there) also impose a great deal of patrolling work upon suitable surface ships. The

176

defence of the range of British Colonies and Protectorates is another task to which we are bound by honour and treaty.

We have to give support to our scientists and surveyors in the South Atlantic and Antarctic and to the communities of the Falklands and South Georgia. We are bound to assist with the curbing of the flood of would-be illegal immigrants into Hong Kong and the cracking down on smuggling and piracy in the South China sea. The list is almost endless. Since the Korean War there has been a long series of operational incidents involving the Royal Navy in its national (rather than NATO) rôle. In 1951, after Egypt had abrogated the 1936 treaty with Britain, units of the Mediterranean Fleet took over Suez Canal operations at Port Said, where there was a general strike, thus ensuring the safe flow of shipping through the canal. This was followed during the four years from 1955 to 1959 by a blockade of the gun runners into Cyprus and valuable support to the British army during the 'Eoka' crisis there. The Suez 'war', which was an Anglo/French naval amphibious operation, took place in the Autumn of 1956 and was followed by the first 'Cod War' with Iceland in 1958/1959 where Navy ships protected British trawlers which were going about their lawful business of fishing off Iceland.

In June 1961 all the signs were that Iraq was about to invade and take over the small but wealthy Kingdom of Kuwait. Britain was invited to come to the country's aid, and a combined force of carriers, surface escorts and amphibious ships landed Royal Marines and other troops and kept the peace, helped by naval air cover from the carriers. Less than a year later, in the Spring of 1962, there were strikes, violence and rioting in British Guiana and the Governor radioed for urgent assistance. This was provided by frigates which landed armed parties ashore—including Dartmouth Officer Cadets under training—and restored order. If events were hotting up in the West Indies they were to get even hotter in the East Indies, where from 1962 to 1966 a running battle, which has been called the Indonesian Confrontation with Malaysia, took place. The Royal Navy and the Royal Marines were involved in the support of the Federal Malaysian Government throughout this period until the summer of 1966, when the Bangkok agreement brought peace. During these four years attempts by the Indonesians to land troops openly or covertly in West Malaysia were constantly blocked by Royal Naval patrolling ships which had a success rate of over ninety per cent, often with back-up carrier aircraft or helicopter support.

During January 1964 President Nyerere had asked the British Government for help in dealing with mutinies in Zanzibar and Dar-es-Salaam. Fortunately, the carrier *Centaur* was at Aden and so she, with attendant escorts, was able to swiftly put in an appearance and quell the mutiny. Her Royal Marines landed by her Wessex helicopters, given air cover by Sea Vixen aircraft. Royal Navy ships continued to call at Zanzibar for some time until the situation was back to normal. In the same part of the world the ten-year Beira patrol took place from 1965 to 1975 in which Navy ships and aircraft stopped blockade runners trying, in defiance of United Nations sanctions, to supply oil to Rhodesia via the Port of Beira in the then Portuguese Colony of Mozambique.

The unrest and violence leading to the withdrawal from Aden very much occupied Royal Navy ships and aircraft in 1967 and 1968. It was in 1967 too that the Gibraltar Guardship was established, consisting of a frigate or similar vessel available at short notice to protect the interests of Gibraltar against infringement by Spanish or other nationals when ships come to anchor in the Bay of Algeciras. This followed the rejection by a referendum held in Gibraltar in 1967 of any proposal to cease to be British territory and to live under Spanish sovereignty. The RN Guardship has continued from 1967 to 1982. A year after its introduction, at the beginning of 1968 an armed revolution took place in Rodriquez, a dependency of Mauritius in the Indian Ocean. In response to the Mauritian Government's appeals for assistance, a destroyer and a ship of the Royal Fleet Auxiliary quelled the rebellion and took the ringleaders to Mauritius for justice. A year later, in the Spring of 1969, the Royal Navy started operations in Northern Ireland. Activities include blockading gun-runners, searching merchant shipping, co-operating closely with the troops and police ashore, using both ships and helicopters. Unfortunately this area of naval operations seems destined to last as long as there is a major security problem in Northern Ireland. A considerable number of naval servicemen, WRNS, ships and helicopters are involved in what is sometimes extremely hazardous duty as I saw for myself when I visited them as a Minister.

In 1972 Guatemala started making threatening noises against its neighbour British Honduras. A major show of naval strength was

178

paraded in the Gulf of Honduras and ever since then a frigate or destroyer known as the 'Belize Guardship' (British Honduras became Belize on independence) has always been stationed with an attendant RFA tanker in the Caribbean, never more than about a day's sailing time away.

The year 1973 saw the second 'Cod War' with differences between the United Kingdom and Iceland over fishing. During this and during the third 'Cod War' (1975-6) our fishing fleets had naval protection. I sincerely hope this ends that particular episode, one which neither the Royal Navy nor the Icelandic fishermen liked and where the ships of the two countries carried the can for the failures of politicians on both sides.

Following the Turkish invasion of Cyprus during the Summer of 1974, the carrier *Hermes* with escort ships and Royal Fleet Auxiliaries evacuated many people and looked after British interests until the situation had reached an uneasy stability.

More lately, from October 1980 onwards, two destroyers or frigates plus supporting Royal Fleet Auxiliaries have been continuously patrolling the Gulf of Oman. This is 'Operation Armilla' safeguarding British and other merchant shipping when it leaves the Persian Gulf and could be threatened by the crossfire of the Iran/Iraq war and the general instability in the area.

These are some of the more important Royal Navy operations of recent years. The minor ones, dealing with hostile acts, piracy, storms, national disasters, insurrections and of course being on the alert to respond to the threat of these, are far too many to list. That is why when people suggest that the Falklands Task force was a 'one-off operation' I reply that in scale it was, although far more Royal Navy ships (six carriers for instance) were involved, for longer periods, in the Korean War. Operations involving risk, skill and using all the flexibility of maritime power have been taking place virtually continuously for thirty years and often several at the same time. All of them were 'one-offs'. If history runs true to form there will be many such 'one-offs' in the months and years ahead.

In each of these we were on our own, defending our national interests or commitments—no one else's; but they add up to a very considerable total. Meanwhile the balance of terror between the major powers does nothing to diminish the number of minor conflicts that take place around the world, indeed quite the reverse.

I would not regard as credible any politician who could promise a reduction of this type of activity in the future unless we became entirely isolationist in this country.

For the Royal Navy to continue to cope in the decades ahead with these operations, skill and professionalism are not enough. We need sufficient 'hulls in the water' so that we can do justice to our NATO commitment and have enough vessels to be able to meet a crisis that affects our interests whenever and wherever it occurs. The Gulf of Oman patrol for example earmarks six ships if two are to be kept on patrol, because two are going home for maintenance while two make preparations and sail out in due course to relieve the third two actually on patrol. The same uncomfortable mathematics will apply to the ships guarding the Falklands in future. Six or nine surface ships plus four or six submarines would be required to maintain three surface ships and two submarines on station permanently in and around the Falklands. These sorts of commitments at long steaming distances from the United Kingdom soon use up all the available ships, manpower and support facilities. There is certainly no way such operations could be undertaken if the 1981 Navy cuts were fully carried out. Nor is there any redundancy in the system, so that we can work with other friendly countries in carrying out sea control at the vital trade 'choke points' and in providing protection that can be called upon for our merchant fleet.

Having established the multiplicity of tasks to be tackled what sort of fleet should we have in order to realistically discharge them? First we continue with our submarine-launched Polaris strategic deterrent until the mid 1990s. The 'Chevaline' improvements to the warhead should keep the missile both effective and credible in the perception of an adversary. We should investigate very much more thoroughly than has been envisaged so far, the possibility of replacing Polaris in due course with submarine-launched nuclear-armed Cruise missiles of an advanced Tomahawk Type. If such a project is found not to be feasible, the cost of Trident must be borne by the Defence budget as a whole—or perhaps it should come from a special strategic fund. It should not distort the whole pattern of our conventional defences by being at the expense of a single service, the Navy. If the economic outlook for Britain and indeed the world is as difficult as the forecasters predict, there must on cost-effective grounds be a major question mark over whether

Trident is now the right system for us.

For sea control, and as a vital core to North Atlantic anti-submarine warfare groups, we now have in firm prospect the three 'Invincible' Class ASW carriers. In due course all will be armed with lightweight Sea Wolf and Phalanx close-in weapon systems. The Falklands crisis has shown that, in an emergency, these ships can carry many more than their normal complement of five Sea Harriers. There is certainly nothing to stop more flight decks with ski-jumps being provided on suitably converted tankers or container ships. The joint UK/USA ARAPAHO project for helicopter and V/STOL decks on merchant ships has much to contribute here and should be accelerated. The fighter direction and command together with control and communications would still be provided by the ASW carrier but the air cover itself could be increased by using merchant ships in this way.

As I have already described the Navy and British industry did a remarkably quick 'lash up' conversion of a Sea King helicopter to carry an airborne warning radar during the Falklands battle. This was better than nothing, but a more sophisticated airborne early warning system is now required as a matter of urgency. If we still had conventional carriers we should undoubtedly go for the American Grumman E-2A 'Hawkeye' twin turboprop early warning aircraft which gives effective radar coverage to a range of up to 240 nautical miles. However these aircraft need a catapult and a conventional deck for take-off and landing and the 'Invincibles' are too small and do not have these features. Therefore they are out for the Royal Navy and we are back to Sea King helicopters fitted with the most appropriate radar.

It now seems to be conventional agreement among almost everyone that only the USA and the USSR can afford conventional carriers. There is no question that they and their aircraft are expensive, as are the frigates needed to give them anti-submarine escort. Yet the French are currently operating two conventional carriers, the *Clemenceau* and the *Foch* using aircraft like the Super Etendard armed with Exocet air-to-surface missiles, together with Crusader interceptor fighters. There are now firm plans for these ships to be replaced by two 35,000 ton nuclear powered carriers named the *Bretagne* and *Provence* respectively, to become operational in the 1990s. Construction of *Bretagne* is due to be started at Brest in 1985.

There is no doubt that a nuclear-powered carrier, with up to forty or so aircraft (mixed fighter, strike, airborne early-warning and electronic warfare), would give Britain a major capability to project maritime power world-wide. Such ships frankly are in a different league from the 'Invincible' Class, but so, of course, is their cost. If, however, significant savings could be made by not proceeding with Trident, but developing a cheaper alternative, then carriers of this size could be a practical proposition. They would be armed with all the appropriate missiles and electronic warfare equipment, and three of such ships, enabling two to be always operational, would form the core of British Carrier Groups, one of which could always be in the North Atlantic and the other available for world-wide deployment for trouble wherever and whenever it arose, acting either in Britain's interests or in concert with her allies. I accept at once that the chances of Britain ever emulating the French Navy are now slim whatever Government is in power. However, if a proper far-reaching review of defence was undertaken and the opportunity costs of the Trident or Tomahawk programmes thoroughly calculated, then we should examine in depth at least the concept of using medium nuclear carriers.

Whatever the outcome of any possible review, however, we shall clearly now have the 'Invincible' Class in service until the next century, and this means buying sufficient Sea Harriers for them and in due course, I hope, a maritime version of the projected supersonic Harrier. When the Sea Harrier is armed with the sea-skimming air-to-surface Sea Eagle anti-ship missile, which is superior in all respects to the Exocet, then the Fleet will pack a larger range punch of significant proportions. While I am considering the subject of aircraft: that splendid workhorse the Sea King helicopter is in need of replacement and I expect that the EH101, a three-engined advanced design-project jointly being produced by Westlands and the Italian Augusta Company, will be its successor at the end of this decade. This helicopter, with its advanced electronic equipment and submarine hunting sonar, will be a powerful addition to the Fleet in the next decade. Armed with Stingray torpedoes it will be a most potent submarine killer. Variants will undoubtedly be used as Commando carriers for operating in amphibious assaults.

As I have already explained, the so called 'increase' in the number of nuclear-powered hunter-killer submarines is actually a decrease of three on the number planned to be in service in the 1990s. I hope that shortfall could be made up since these boats, together with their smaller conventional diesel/electronic counterparts, have a number of important rôles. Fitted with a variety of listening sonar devices, they can hunt enemy submarines or surface ships and destroy them with long-range guided 'Tigerfish' torpedoes. These are to be replaced, at the end of the decade, by the very fast highly advanced 'Spearfish' torpedo; these are really underwater guided missiles.

In addition some of our submarines will carry the sub-to-surface missile 'Harpoon' which can knock out a surface ship and has a seventy mile range. I hope, as I have said, very much that we can seriously consider fitting our nuclear hunter-killer submarines and our new 2400 class diesel/electronic boats with Tomahawk Cruise missiles. These can be fired from vertical launches and do not interfere with the torpedoes carried on board. These missiles have ranges varying from two hundred to nearly two thousand miles and can be armed with high explosive or nuclear warheads. As I have already explained at some length, this is a way that our Fleet could have formidable nuclear capability without many of Trident's problems and costs.

We have so far looked at the exotic and expensive end of the spectrum. But all this becomes so much verbiage if the numbers and quality of surface escorts are not adequate to discharge their many tasks. The high quality heart of this part of the Fleet is the class of Type 22 frigates armed with Exocet and Sea Wolf missiles, Lynx helicopters, Stingray anti-submarine torpedoes and excellent radar, sonar and communications facilities. I believe that we need to keep building versions of this Class through the 1980s as the Navy's First Rate frigate; the replacement vessels for those sunk in the Falklands must be Type 22 frigates.

They will be backed up by the cheaper and smaller Type 23 that will incorporate lightweight Sea Wolf and a very quiet electric drive to its propellers so that it can operate new listening sonar devices to detect submarines. The main engines and generators should be mounted on acoustic rafts also for quietness; these will probably be the new Rolls-Royce Maritime Spey gas turbine. The Type 23 will have a hangar and will be able to operate the EH101 anti-submarine helicopters at long ranges in Mid Atlantic. Unfortunately it now looks as if these frigates will not enter service until 1989 at the earliest and they will need to be ordered at the rate of three or four every year to maintain fleet numbers as old ships are sold or scrapped. I regard the Type 23 as the Navy's Second Rate frigate.

I hope that in both frigates it will be possible to fit, when it is developed, British Aerospace's new ship-launched 'fire and forget' sea-skimming heavyweight missile, the P5T. This is based on the Sea Eagle air-launched missile and would give substantial firepower to a comparatively small surface ship. It should be available to coincide with the introduction into service of the Type 23 frigate and is the next generation on from the existing ship-mounted Exocet missiles, currently fitted in Type 21 and 22 Class frigates.

The irreducible number of frigates and destroyers that should be in operational service should be fifty, and there should be an additional fifteen in refit, as training or trial ships or in reserve, totalling sixty-five in all. I stress that these are minimum figures. The forty-two operational frigates and destroyers proposed in the 1981 White Paper, less several more refitting, would reduce the force to about thirty-five in practical terms and I know of no way that such a number of ships could discharge all our NATO commitments, let alone the other purely national tasks that I have described. In case anyone thinks I am being wildly extravagant or unrealistic it is perhaps worth noting that when the Conservative Government entered office in May 1979, there were fifty-four destroyers and frigates in operational service, plus fourteen refitting or in reserve.

A lesson to be learned from the Falklands (or indeed from Admiral Gorshkov) is that radars, sonars, weapons, communications and electronic equipment must be kept sufficiently up-to-date to deal with the threat. A ship entering service in the mid-1980s fitted with 1960s-designed weapons systems which have not been improved, or had their known deficiencies removed, will do little for our naval strength and may ensure the crew has an early and unnecessary watery grave. Radar sets that have limited range, poor definition or can be easily jammed are a menace. A lack of modern electronic counter measures to deal with missiles from second or third line navies, destroys the credibility of the protection that the Royal Navy gives to British and other merchant shipping within and without NATO. It is clear that to bring a complete weapon system up to date not only makes sense but is also invariably quicker and cheaper than building anew. Interestingly the 1981 Defence Review encouraged the pulling out of a lot of equipment from the twelve year old Nimrod I maritime patrol aircraft, replacing it with new and expensive electronics like Searchwater radar and calling it a Nimrod II! At the same time however it proposed to discontinue the modernisation of the twelve year old Leander frigates and the fitting of them with Exocet and Sea Wolf missiles...

The fleet must be supplemented by other important vessels. For the defence against mining of UK ports and the international 'choke points', new cheap single-rôle minehunters are required to back up the very sophisticated and very expensive GRP 'Hunt' Class mine countermeasure vessels. The new cheap 'trawler' type minesweepers for the RNR are not only vital to deal with certain types of mine, they are necessary too to give sea-time and training to the Reserves.

The inexpensive long-endurance diesel-driven 'Castle' Class corvettes (a better name than 'offshore patrol vessels') have already performed extremely well in the South Atlantic. Variants of the design can be fitted with different gun, missile or anti-submarine weapons systems and their large flight decks enable them to operate Lynx or Sea King helicopters. I believe that these ships could be developed for a variety of rôles for the Royal Navy and have a reasonable export potential too. With a crew of fifty or thereabouts, a range with their diesels of 8000 miles, they give the Navy an opportunity to have inexpensive quality with a punch, using commercial weapons and fire control and radar systems.

In a democracy however, and this is a most important point, resources for defence are always going to be constrained. If the Navy that I wish to see is achieved, a revolution in Ministry procurement will have to come first. There will have to be a blitz on committees, a target of reducing by fifty per cent the 'definition' and design time and a freeze on the design once it is agreed. 'Gold plating', as it is called, must be out. If equipment or components can be supplied by British industry then they must be bought here. If British industry cannot provide this we must try to purchase within NATO. But the old service habit of a unique, expensive and complex design for virtually every nut and bolt is just not on in the future. Naval designers must work much closer together with industry right from the start of each project and thereby save time, talent and much money.

There are other fringe or experimental areas of naval activity

185

that Defence cuts have forced the Admiralty Board to abandon. I have been impressed by the potential of large jet-foils armed with surface-to-surface short or medium range Cruise missiles. The Royal Navy were not even allowed to complete the trials of their first fast and highly manoeuverable jetfoil HMS *Speedy*, before she was paid off for disposal in April 1982, notwithstanding an offer by her makers, Boeings, to make a significant financial contribution to the cost of completing the trials programme. At about the same time, and for the same reason, the Hovercraft Trials Unit was disbanded, although many people consider that these craft have an important future in mine countermeasures work, among other tasks. Within the Navy's ambit either a Royal Fleet Auxiliary or a Royal Navy repair ship along the lines of the *Stena Sea Speed* which I have already described clearly appears to be a high priority. If we use the precepts that I have been propounding we ought to buy a commercially designed and built ship and spend the absolute minimum in adapting it to service use.

A fleet along these lines could meet our NATO and our national obligations—just. But the 1981 Defence Review will need rethinking by Mr Nott's successors on three key areas of policy. Firstly there should not, with these numbers of ships, be any requirement at all for service redundancies, whether forced or voluntary. The Navy and the Royal Marines together should maintain a strength of about 78,000 officers and other ranks. In 1982 the strength was 73,000 and due to drop substantially during the rest of the 1980s.

Secondly, the training of service personnel should not all be carried out at sea and money should not be saved by closing many of the shore establishments as the 1981 Review envisages. Such a policy means that a ship is never at one hundred per cent operational efficiency because a significant number of its crew are unskilled and under training, or the experienced ones are spending too much of their time teaching. Savings and greater efficiency can always be achieved in any organisation. The more extensive use of simulators and modern teaching aids can make training interesting, realistic and relevant. To make a major change is a very high risk policy which, I believe, we shall bitterly regret.

Thirdly, a Fleet which can meet our commitments and keep itself up-to-date needs modern skilled dockyard and logistic support. New radar systems or missile launchers simply cannot be fitted at just

186

any commercial shipyard. These highly sophisticated operations require very special skills and equipment. If Chatham and Gibraltar are closed and Portsmouth is run right down such facilities would not remain in sufficient quality at the remaining yards, Devonport and Rosyth. I cannot stress too strongly that there are major reasons of national security for, at the very least, retaining the nuclear refitting capacity at Chatham and not reducing Portsmouth or closing Gibraltar. I believe that the financial savings at the end of the day, if these closures go through, will prove to be largely illusory—but the damaging effect on both the surface and submarine fleet will not. By the same token it does not make sense to destroy many of the supporting stores depots; or to dispose of vital RFA ships. These are needed to give essential support for the Navy so that if a supreme effort is needed the system will work quickly and efficiently as it did on that first April weekend in 1982.

I must emphasise that in this book's previous chapters, with their various stories, prejudices and opinions, I am not simply arguing for a stop to the present eccentric policy of cutting back hard on the Navy, a policy which I believe to be profoundly un-Conservative, but that I am trying to show that our defences, our trade, our influence abroad, our energy and fishing interests all rely upon the understanding, development and proper deployment of maritime power. All my experience as a professional Naval Officer, businessman, Minister and now ex-Minister lead me to no other conclusion.

It is no good having the strongest Navy in Western Europe if our shipyards go bankrupt and our merchant fleets dwindle to nothing. It is no good if our Government relies upon the geographical blessing of off-shore gas and oil if we cannot at all times properly defend the installations. It is no good giving assurances of security to our friends in different parts of the world, if we deny ourselves the means of discharging our obligations. It is no good having a thriving mercantile marine carrying our exports and imports to and from the world's markets if our ships cannot be protected from those countries who may wish to do us damage, without risking a world conflagration.

We have to remember that we make a key contribution to the North Atlantic Treaty Organisation and in so doing have to face and contain, with our allies, the largest and most powerful navy the world has ever seen, and this means sea control with desperately stretched resources.

I want to see a greater understanding of the meaning and a more corporate approach to the use of maritime power by government and industry. The defence, mercantile, industrial, commercial, foreign policy, fishing, energy and trade aspects must all be considered together, for all affect, for good or ill, national security and national prosperity. We have a highly developed island economy, world-wide interests and major national resources lying under the seas around us, and depredations in the strength of the Royal Navy must cease now if we are to continue to be adequately protected.

The sixteen years from 1966 to 1982 have shown a sometimes slow, but always steady retreat from a strong national maritime strategy. The fact that the Navy and the Royal Marines have achieved so much, ranging from the Indonesian confrontation to the recapture of Port Stanley in that period, is in spite of, rather than because of, politicians of all parties. Our American allies have now called a halt to the lack of understanding, the indecision and the haemorrhaging of their own maritime capability just in time. Have we in the United Kingdom the wisdom to do likewise?

I started this book by telling of the resignation of a Navy Minister. Let me finish by quoting the last three sentences of the speech that led to my dismissal as Navy Minister when at Tenterden on 15th May 1980 I told my audience:

> Let me leave the last word with another famous Russian. It was Solzhenitsyn who said: 'The threat lies not so much in the capabilities of its enemies as in the indifference of the West.' If that has been true in parts of Europe we must not allow it to become true here.

References

1   *Daily Telegraph* of 21st February, 1966
2   *Hansard* Col. 1790, 7th March, 1966
3   *Hansard* Col. 1792, 7th March, 1966
4   *Hansard* Col. 1794, 7th March, 1966
5   *Hansard* Col. 635, 25th January, 1968
6   *Sea Power of the State*, p. 179
7   *The Soviet Navy*, Ed. Commander M. G. Saunders, 1958, p. 100
8   *Sea Power of the State*, p. 277
9   *Sea Power of the State*, p. 218
10 *Cold War Navy*, Chpt. 18 p. 8 by Richard K. Smith. Published by Lulejian and assocs, 1976
11 *Hansard* Col. 1971
12 *Sea Power of the State*, p. 42
13 *Hansard* Col. 1818, 19th June, 1980
14 *Hansard* (written answer) Col. 148, 6th August, 1980
15 Command 8212, April 1981
16 *Hansard* Cols 180-183, 19th May, 1981
17 Command 8288
18 *Hansard* Col. 27, 29th March, 1982
19 General Council of British Shipping, briefing note, 29th June, 1982
20 *Hansard* Col. 108, 19th July, 1982
21 *Navy International*, May 1982, p. 1069

Selected Bibliography

Janes Fighting Ships

The Decline of British Sea Power, Desmond Welton, Janes, 1982

Statement on the Defence Estimates for various years up to 1982

Proceedings of the U.S. Naval Institute, Annapolis, U.S.A.

Official year books of the Republic of South Africa

Annual Report to Congress, 1983, by U.S. Secretary of Defense

The Russian Navy, Eric Morris, Hamish Hamilton, 1977

The U.S. Navy, Nathan Miller, American Heritage Publishing Co., 1977

The Falklands Conflict, Dobson, Miller and Payne, Coronet Books, 1982

British Warships and Auxiliaries, 1980, 81, 82, Maritime Books

Flashing Blades over the Sea, Lt-Cdr. Milne., Maritime Books, 1980

A Sailor's Odyssey, Admiral of the Fleet Viscount Cunningham of Hyndhope, Hutchinson, 1951

Lloyds Register of Shipping

Sea Fisheries Statistical Tables, Ministry of Agriculture Fisheries and Food

The Sea Power of the State, Admiral S.G. Gorshkov, Pergamon Press, 1979

The Nation and the Navy, Christopher Lloyd, Cresset Press, 1954

Sea Power, Admiral of the Fleet Lord Hill-Norton and John Dekker, Faber and Faber, 1982

The Soviet Navy, Ed. Cdr. M.G. Saunders, Weidenfeld and Nicholson, 1958

Index